PagePlus
Made Simple

GW00506633

Made Simple *Computer Books*

● easy to follow   ● jargon free   ● practical   ● task based   ● easy steps

Thousands of people have already discovered that the **MADE SIMPLE** series gives them what they want *fast!* These are the books for you if you want to **learn quickly what's essential** and **how** to do things with a particular piece of software. You are:

● **a Secretary** or **temp** who wants to **get the job done**, **quickly** and **efficiently**

● **a Manager**, without the time to learn all about the software but who wants to **produce** letters, memos, reports or **spreadsheets**

● someone **working from home**, who needs a **self-teaching** approach, that gives **results fast**, with the least confusion.

For **clarity** and **simplicity**, the **MADE SIMPLE** Computer Books stand above all others.

This **best selling** series is in your **local bookshop now**, or in case of difficulty, contact:

Reed Book Services Ltd., Orders Dept, PO Box 5, Rushden, Northants, NN10 9YX. Tel 01933 58521. Fax 01933 50284. Credit card sales 01933 410511.

Series titles:

AmiPro for Windows	Moira Stephen	0 7506 2067 6
Excel for Windows	Stephen Morris	0 7506 2070 6
Lotus 1-2-3 (DOS)	Ian Robertson	0 7506 2066 8
MS-DOS	Ian Sinclair	0 7506 2069 2
MS-Works for Windows	P. K. McBride	0 7506 2065 X
Windows 3.1	P. K. McBride	0 7506 2072 2
Word for Windows	Keith Brindley	0 7506 2071 4
WordPerfect (DOS)	Stephen Copestake	0 7506 2068 4
Access for Windows	Moira Stephen	0 7506 2309 8
The Internet	P.K.McBride	0 7506 2311 X
Quicken for Windows	Stephen Copestake	0 7506 2308 X
WordPerfect for Windows	Keith Brindley	0 7506 2310 1
Lotus 123 (5.0) for Windows	Stephen Morris	0 7506 2307 1
Multimedia	Simon Collin	0 7506 2314 4
Pageplus for Windows	Ian Sinclair	0 7506 2312 8
PowerPoint	Moira Stephen	0 7506 2420 5
Hard drives	Ian Robertson	0 7506 2313 6
Windows 95	P.K.McBride	0 7506 2306 3

PagePlus
Made Simple

Ian Sinclair

MADE SIMPLE
BOOKS

Made Simple
An imprint of Butterworth-Heinemann Ltd
Linacre House, Jordan Hill, Oxford OX2 8DP

ℛ   A member of the Reed Elsevier plc group

OXFORD   LONDON   BOSTON
MUNICH   NEW DELHI   SINGAPORE   SYDNEY
TOKYO   TORONTO   WELLINGTON

First published 1995
© Ian Sinclair 1995

TRADEMARKS/REGISTERED TRADEMARKS
Computer hardware and software brand names mentioned in this book are protected
by their respective trademarks and are acknowledged.

British Library Cataloguing in Publication Data
A catalogue record for this book is available from the British Library

ISBN 0 7506 2312 8

✿ Typeset by P.K.McBride, Southampton
Archtype, Bash Casual, Cotswold and Gravity fonts from Advanced Graphics Ltd
Icons designed by Sarah Ward © 1994
Printed and bound in Great Britain by Scotprint, Musselburgh, Scotland

Contents

Preface

The computer is about as simple as a spacecraft, and who ever let an untrained spaceman loose? You pick up a manual that weighs more than your birth-weight, open it and find that its written in computerspeak. You see messages on the screen that look like code and the thing even makes noises. No wonder that you feel it's your lucky day if everything goes right. What do you do if everything goes wrong? Give up.

Training helps. Being able to type helps. Experience helps. This book helps, by providing training and assisting with experience. It can't help you if you always manage to hit the wrong keys, but it can tell you which are the right ones and what to do when you hit the wrong ones. After some time, even the dreaded manual will start to make sense, just because you know what the writers are wittering on about.

Computing is not black magic. You don't need luck or charms, just a bit of understanding. The problem is that the programs that are used nowadays look simple but aren't. Most of them are crammed with features you don't need – but how do you know what you don't need? This book shows you what is essential and guides you through it. You will know how to make an action work and why. The less essential bits can wait – and once you start to use a program with confidence you can tackle these bits for yourself.

The writers of this series have all been through it. We know your time is valuable, and you don't want to waste it. You don't buy books on computer subjects to read jokes or be told that you are a dummy. You want to find what you need and be shown how to achieve it. Here, at last, you can.

1 Starting up

Starting PagePlus

You must have installed PagePlus 3.0 correctly, using the INSTALL program on the first of the set of six floppy disks. If you have bought the complete set of PagePlus programs and files on CD-ROM, follow the instructions for the CD-ROM set.

The easiest way of starting PagePlus 3.0 is to double-click on its icon. This is in the Serif Applications set contained in your Program Manager.

Basic steps

1 Double-click on the **Serif Applications** group in your **Program Manager** display.

2 Now double-click on the **PagePlus** icon in this group
PagePlus 3.0

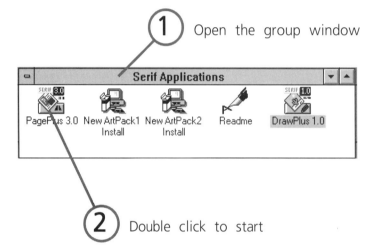

(1) Open the group window

(2) Double click to start

Take note

If you change to Windows 95, you will find that actions that used to need double-clicking now need just a single click

Tip

If words like clicking and dragging are new to you, you should read the companion book, Windows Made Simple.

Features

The **Toolbox** is the fast way of using PagePlus action commands by pointing and clicking

When you first start using PagePlus 3.0 you will see the page appear with the Serif Welcome sheet. Click on any of the four panels that offer information and assistance, mostly concerned with registering for technical support.

The **Menu** is the slower way of controlling PagePlus, but easier to understand at the start.

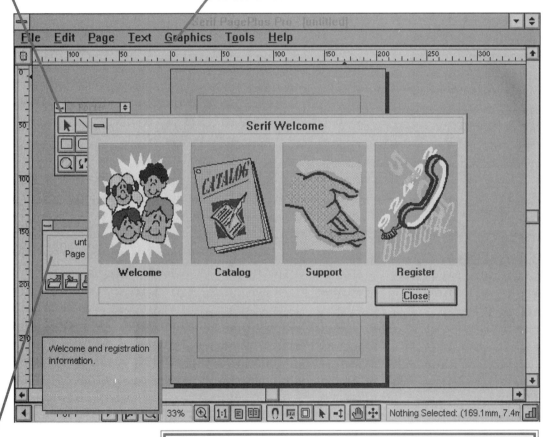

The **Changebar** is the fast way to alter the appearance of text by changing, for example, fonts and letter sizes

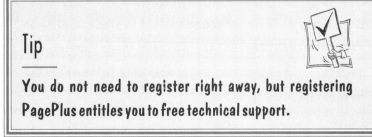

Tip

You do not need to register right away, but registering PagePlus entitles you to free technical support.

Startup Assistant

Startup Assistant is a display that makes it easier for you to sort out what you want when you switch on PagePlus. Like all other DTP programs, PagePlus offers a bewildering variety of commands, and by focusing your choice at the start, the Assistant helps you to concentrate on the essentials.

(1) Click one to select

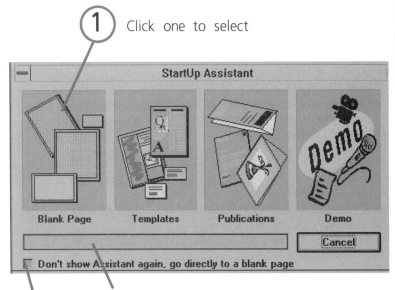

Blank Page   Templates   Publications   Demo

Reminder message

(2) Check if Assistant not wanted

1 The cursor can be placed on any of the four options. They allow you to use a new page, follow an existing pattern (template), recall an existing publication, or watch a demonstration.

❏ The action of each option is explained on the message line.

2 Check the **Don't display Assistant** box, to prevent this display from appearing again.

Take note

If you know what sort of page you want to produce, click on Templates. You can then choose a ready-made template as a pattern for the page layout, and concentrate on the words and images that you want to use.

Tip

Keep the Assistant until you are more experienced, when you can opt to start with a fresh page each time.

Templates

1 Select the category of publication.

2 Select a named **Template** from the set.

❑ You will see a preview of the template

3 Click **OK**

Much of the work you are likely to want to create can use a template, either directly or with small modifications. If, when you have more experience, you create something that you might want to use again you can save it as a template of your own. PagePlus contains a directory for saving your own templates.

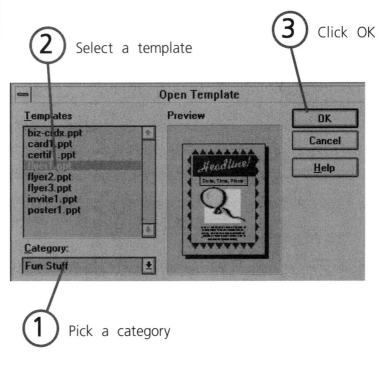

Tip

The PagePlus Business set of templates contains expenses, planners, fax sheets, invoices, purchase orders and quotes which can all be used almost unchanged to meet most of your business requirements.

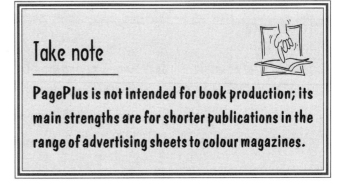

Take note

PagePlus is not intended for book production; its main strengths are for shorter publications in the range of advertising sheets to colour magazines.

Using a template

The Invoice template has been used as an example here. It would take a considerable time to create from scratch, but it is comparatively easy to alter to your own requirements once you have some experience of PagePlus. Other templates are easier to alter, and they save a considerable amount of time as compared to creating your own.

② Edit as needed

① Click for a tip

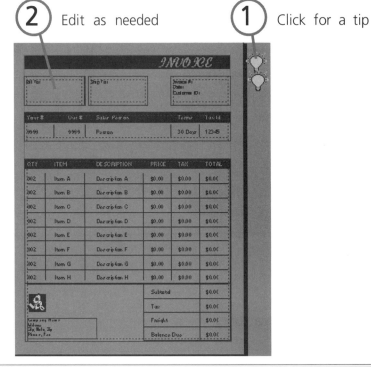

Basic steps

1 The light-bulbs indicate tips. Click on one to see the help it offers. You can drag the symbols around or remove them as you wish.

2 The spaces are labelled with standard items like **Bill To** and **Ship To**. Edit these to your own requirements.

❑ When you edit a standard template like this, **save** the edited version as one of your own templates.

Tip

If you are going to use templates that involve money, you will have to change all the $ into £. This is not difficult, but you need to switch to Professional Level, see later.

Take Note

You can alter a template in easy stages, saving the file (as your template) after each change. If it all starts to look scrambled you can either use the Undo command in the File menu, or you can abandon the page and load in the last version you saved

Basic steps

1 Click on the text icon **A** in the Toolbox.

2 Click at the end of the text you want to change and use the **[Backspace]** key to remove it. Now type in your own heading.

3 Repeat this with the other lettering you need to change.

4 Now save the result as a template of your own - use the **File** menu and select **Save As**. Select **Template** as the type of file, and select the **PP30 \ Template \ Mytemplt** directory. Type a name such as *MYFAX*, and click on the **OK** button to save it.

Take Note

See later for more details of saving publication and template files

Editing

Here's how to adapt a simple template. This is the Fax template of PagePlus as it first appears. Using a few simple steps, you can adapt this for your own needs. To edit text you must first select the Edit tool in the Toolbox. Later we'll see how the images in a page can also be edited or replaced.

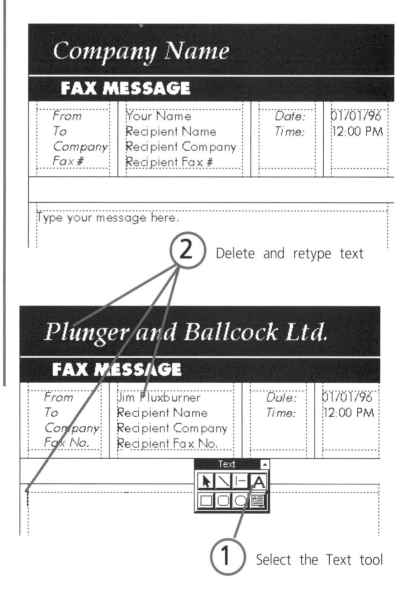

(2) Delete and retype text

(1) Select the Text tool

Summary

❑ PagePlus 3.0 is ideal for creating short publications. It is also useful for long but straightforward text, such as a novel.

❑ PagePlus uses **standard Windows methods**, and you must be familiar with actions such as clicking, double-clicking, and dragging.

❑ When the program is installed on your hard drive, you can **start** it by double-clicking on its icon in the Serif Applications group.

❑ When you start PagePlus for the first time, the Welcome message will remind you to **register** for technical service.

❑ The **Starting Assistant** provides you with a simple choice of actions each time you start PagePlus

❑ **Templates** provide ready-made patterns for your own work, and save considerable time and effort.

❑ The **Toolbox** is a very important part of PagePlus, allowing you to control actions such as text editing.

❑ You can edit text in a template.

❑ When you alter a template, use the **Save As** option in the **File** menu to save the new template, with a new filename, for future use.

2   Screen appearance

The page

The PagePlus page is shown on the screen surrounded by a space called the Pasteboard. You can do rough work and try out ideas on the pasteboard, and then drag your work on to the page area.

The Toolbox, Changebar and Quickhelp boxes are called palettes, and they 'float', meaning that you can drag them wherever you want them on screen.

Tip

Watch the Quickhelp window as you move the cursor. Help messages appear for each item the cursor passes over.

(1) Changebar (2) Toolbox (3) Page area

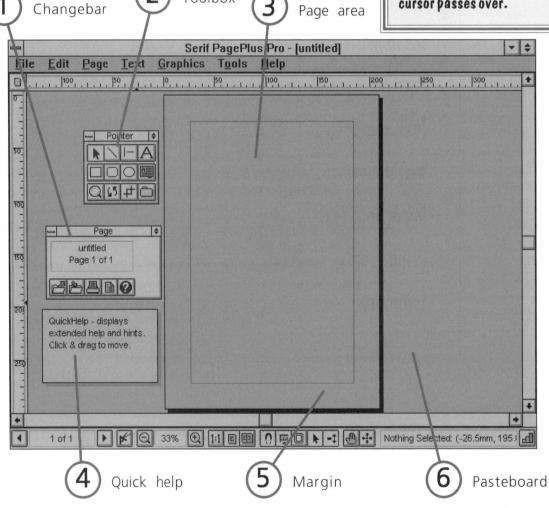

(4) Quick help (5) Margin (6) Pasteboard

Basic steps

1 Click on the text icon in Toolbox

2 Cursor shows where text will appear. Type your text.

3 The width indicator shows the boundaries of the text.

4 The 'handles' indicate that this paragraph is selected and can be moved or its size altered.

There are several ways of placing text on a page, and two main ways of arranging the text. The two ways of arranging text are as unframed or framed text, and in this page we'll look at unframed text.

Unframed in this sense just means that the text is placed starting wherever you click the mouse, and extending for as far as the ruler markings indicate. The small line cursor shows where each typed character will appear.

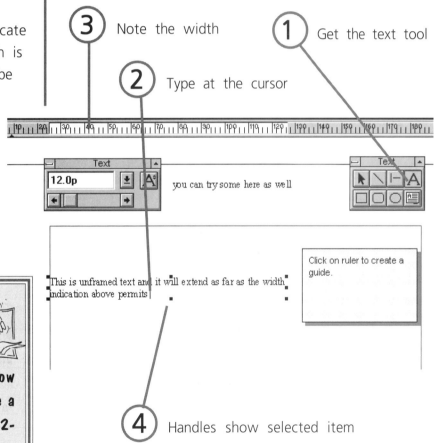

③ Note the width

① Get the text tool

② Type at the cursor

④ Handles show selected item

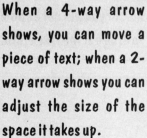

Take note

When a 4-way arrow shows, you can move a piece of text; when a 2-way arrow shows you can adjust the size of the space it takes up.

Text space

The text size, as you normally see it, will be very small on screen, and you can zoom up (magnify) the image by clicking on the magnifying-glass icon ⊕ at the foot of the screen. Click again to increase the size, or click on the ⊖ icon. These icons are shown below

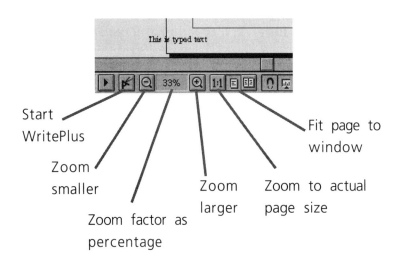

Start WritePlus

Zoom smaller

Zoom factor as percentage

Zoom larger

Zoom to actual page size

Fit page to window

When you enter freetext like this you can fix the text width by dragging the ruler-mark (a small triangle). You can also re-size the text selection box, see later.

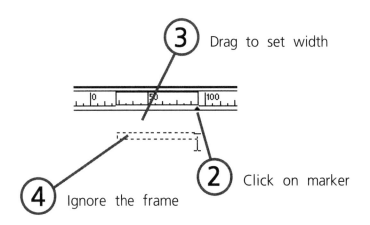

③ Drag to set width

④ Ignore the frame

② Click on marker

1 Place the cursor where you want to place the left hand side of the text.

2 Hold the [Shift] key and click on the triangle marker.

3 Drag the marker until it indicates the text width that you want.

4 You will see a small frame appear as you drag the width - you can ignore this.

Tip

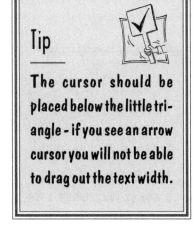

The cursor should be placed below the little triangle - if you see an arrow cursor you will not be able to drag out the text width.

Basic steps

1 Click on the **WritePlus** icon 🖋, or double-click with the text tool selected.

2 Type your text.

3 Use the **Bold**, *Italic* or Underline effects on text as required

4 Use **Cut**, **Copy** and **Paste** as required

5 Use **Find and Replace** on long text if you want to make changes throughout the text.

6 Click on the **spell-checker** to check the words in your text.

Typing text directly into the page is not a good idea unless you are entering only a few words. If you can see the whole page on the screen, the characters are likely to be too small to read. If you look at a magnified version, you cannot see the whole page.

PagePlus contains WritePlus, a word-processor that allows you to prepare text without straining your eyes. If you are familiar with any form of word-processor you will find WritePlus easy to use,.

Select text by dragging the cursor over it before you use text effects such as Bold, Italic, or Underline. You also need to select text to use Cut or Copy.

To use the spelling checker, place the cursor at the start of the text and click on the speller icon.

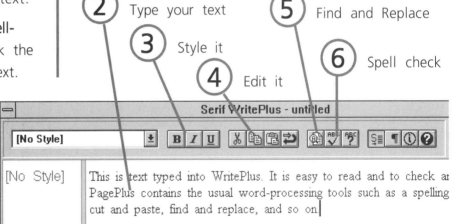

2 Type your text
5 Find and Replace
3 Style it
6 Spell check
4 Edit it

Serif WritePlus - untitled

[No Style] | **B** *I* U

[No Style] | This is text typed into WritePlus. It is easy to read and to check an PagePlus contains the usual word-processing tools such as a spelling cut and paste, find and replace, and so on.

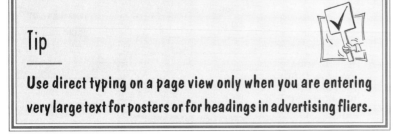

Tip

Use direct typing on a page view only when you are entering very large text for posters or for headings in advertising fliers.

Importing text

If you already have text that has been prepared on a word-processor, or if you prefer to use your favourite word-processor, you can import such text as a file into PagePlus.

PagePlus can import a wide variety of word-processor files, including the Notepad and Write files of Windows. The full list, (with usual extension letters) is:

ASCII text (TXT)   AmiPro (SAM)   MS Word (DOC)

MultiMate (DOC)   Notepad (TXT)   ProWrite (DOC)

Rich Text (RTF)   WordPerfect (DOC)

WordStar (DOC)   Write (WRI)

Basic steps

1 Click on the **File** menu, and then on **Import Text**

2 Select the **Type** of word-processor file from the list

3 Select the **Directory** that contains the files you want

4 Type a **File Name** OR Select one from the list

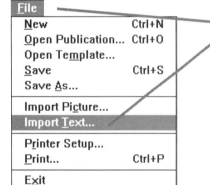

Select File – Import Text

③ Set the directory

④ Type or select a name

② Select a type

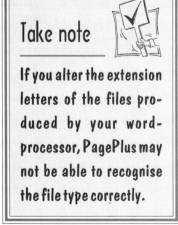

Take note

If you alter the extension letters of the files produced by your word-processor, PagePlus may not be able to recognise the file type correctly.

Basic steps

1 Click on the Frame tool 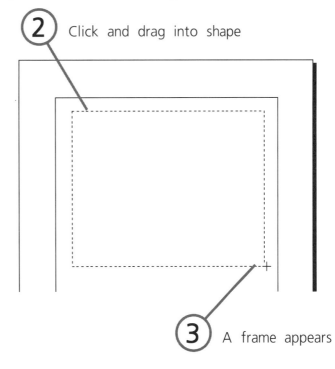 in the Toolbox

2 Click on the starting point and drag out the frame on the page.

3 The frame will appear as a dotted box on the screen view of the page.

❏ When a frame appears, the default is for two columns – one of the most common uses for a text frame. You can alter the number of columns from the **Page** menu, using the **Columns** option.

A frame is a box drawn in dotted lines. This frame does not appear on the printed page, but it defines on the screen the area that text can occupy. Using a frame for text ensures that it can be positioned exactly where you want it, particularly if your page includes graphics, columns, or different sections of text.

When you create a frame, the Frame Assistant will appear, so that you can proceed to import text, type text directory, use WritePlus, or add more frames. Added frames are linked, so that text that has filled one frame will be automatically poured into the next one in the linking order, even if the frames are not close to each other. You can opt to dispense with the Frame Assistant once you are familiar with PagePlus.

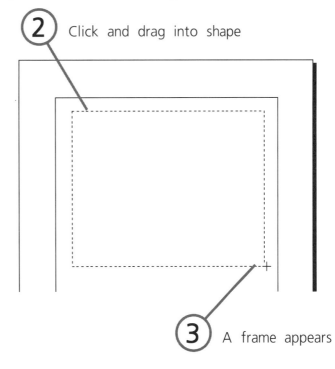

② Click and drag into shape

③ A frame appears

Take note

A frame determines how wide and how deep your text can be - you do not need to drag ruler marks.

Summary

- ❑ The **screen display** shows the page with its margins on the Pasteboard, and with the Toolbox, Changebar and Quickhelp visible.

- ❑ All **text entry** starts by selecting the text tool.

- ❑ The **Pasteboard** can be used to assemble text and drawings before they are placed on the page.

- ❑ **Unframed text** can be placed anywhere on the page or on the pasteboard.

- ❑ The **width of unframed text** can be altered by dragging the cursor along the page - the ruler line shows the limits.

- ❑ Text typed on the page is usually too small to see clearly. **Zoom in** with the magnifying-glass icons.

- ❑ Only small amounts of text, preferably in a large size, should be typed directly.

- ❑ PagePlus contains a word-processor, **WritePlus**. This has a spelling checker, cut and paste, and find and replace actions. (See Sections 8 and 9.)

- ❑ **Text can be imported** from the files created by other word-processors. Imported text is more suited for the use of frames.

- ❑ **Text can be written** in a frame. This determines the width and depth of the text, and a frame can be linked to another so that text that overflows from one into the next.

- ❑ The default frame uses two **columns**, but this can be altered with the Page – Columns command.

3 Settings and printing

Page specification

The page is the most important unit of a PagePlus publication, and it's time now to look at how you specify a page, before anything is placed upon it.

The first point to consider is the page size. For some kinds of work you would make this the same as the paper size (the sheet) that the printer uses, but this is not inevitable. You might, for example, want to print book pages in the size that printers call Demy 8vo, but use A4 sheets in your printer. In that case you would specify the Demy 8vo page size for PagePlus, A4 for the printer, and opt to use crop marks to show where the sheets should be trimmed.

Another example is booklet production, printing on to sheets that are then folded and stapled. As we shall see, PagePlus allows you to prepare pages in sequence and automatically print for folded copy – no more scratching your head and wondering which page number needs to go on which part of the larger sheet.

1 Click on **Page Size** from the **Page** menu.

2 Select from the list of common sizes - the UK version of PagePlus includes the A3, A4 and A5 sizes.

3 Click on **Orientation** to specify which way up the page will be read.

4 Choose **Tall** (Portrait) or **Wide** (Landscape).

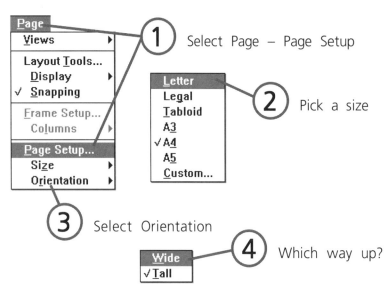

1 Select Page – Page Setup

2 Pick a size

3 Select Orientation

4 Which way up?

Tip

If you want to use other sizes, use the Custom option. This allows you to type in page size, margin size and specify the use of columns to your own specification. The page size that you specify need not be the same as the printer sheet size.

Option choices

1 Specify your units, with a choice of millimetres, centimetres, inches and tenths, printer's picas and points, plus two less common units, ciceros and didots.

2 Decide what elements you want to **Display** - the defaults as shown here are useful and you should keep them ticked until you have had more experience.

3 The **Options** set has two defaults. Do not alter this set until you have more experience.

4 Select your **Language** version from US, or two varieties of UK English with *ise* or *ize* endings to words like customise and standardise.

General Preferences

The **General Preferences** option from the **Tools** menu allows you to specify some important options and to use them as defaults from that point onwards.

The **Don't overset text** option is seldom required, and its effect is not obvious. The **Metafiles on Clipboard** option should also be left unchanged.

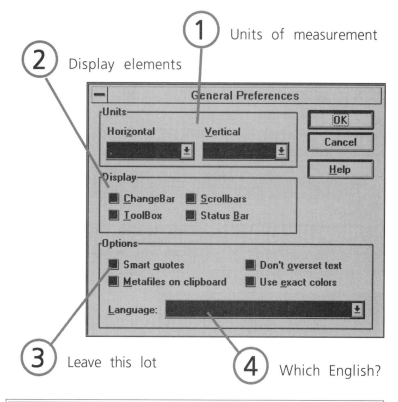

① Units of measurement

② Display elements

③ Leave this lot

④ Which English?

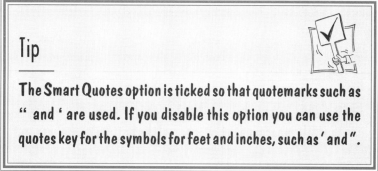

Tip

The Smart Quotes option is ticked so that quotemarks such as " and ' are used. If you disable this option you can use the quotes key for the symbols for feet and inches, such as ' and ".

Other preferences

The **Tools** menu **Preferences** options can be clicked for the **Ease of Use Preferences**, which are in three groups listed here, right.

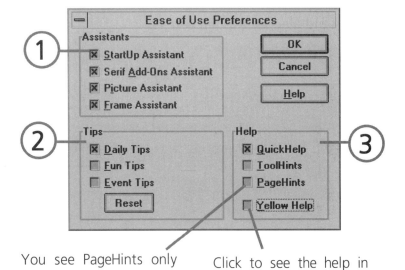

You see PageHints only if you have typed them into a publication.

Click to see the help in more visible yellow boxes.

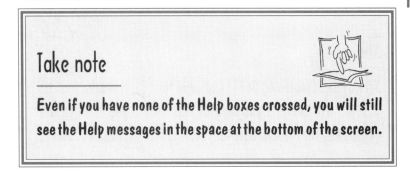

Help is always here

1 **Assistants**. The crossed items show the actions for which an Assistant display appears when you use the action. You might want to dispense with the Startup assistant, but retain the others.

2 **Tips**. Only the **Daily** tips are shown crossed here. You might prefer to cross the **Event** tips, which provide help when you most need it. The **Fun** tips will challenge your sense of humour.

3 The **Help** tips allow up to four Help "stickers" to appear at any one time, and while you are learning to use PagePlus you should opt to use all four.

Take note

Even if you have none of the Help boxes crossed, you will still see the Help messages in the space at the bottom of the screen.

Frame Defaults

1 The frame **Margins** are the distances between the edges of the frame and the page (paper) margins. The default is 2.5 mm, about 0.1 inch.

2 The default number of **Columns** is 2. Change this to 1 if you want to work with, for example, book pages.

3 The gap between columns (the gutter) has a default of 5.1 mm. If you are using multiple columns you can alter this to whatever values you find more appropriate.

The **Defaults** options in the **Tools** menu should also be left alone for now. One possible exception is the **Frame Defaults**, because if you use frames for text, you may want to alter frame spacing and number of columns.

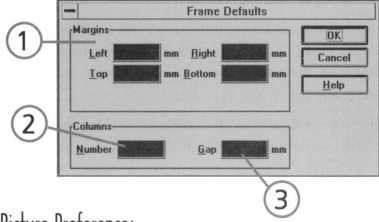

Picture Preferences

This box can be left alone. Its defaults are very sensible ones that you will not need to alter until you have had more experience. The only point to watch is that the default of **Always Link Pictures** means that the page files should be kept with the picture files - see later for more details of linking and embedding.

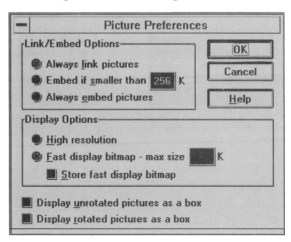

21

Levels of use

When you have altered the settings of Defaults and Preferences you will usually want to use these same settings in future. If so, click on the **Save Settings** option of the **Tools** menu, and specify in the list that appears the settings you want to retain.

The other important option in the **Tools** menu is **PagePlus Level**. PagePlus can be used at three levels, termed Intro, Publisher and Professional. You can switch levels at any time, and the reason is to avoid confusion.

If you work at Intro level, PagePlus looks simpler because advanced options are hidden from you, and the tips and help notes are set for maximum assistance. When you move to higher levels, more facilities are available, so that menus and palettes become larger.

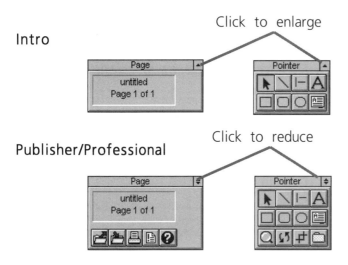

Intro

Click to enlarge

Publisher/Professional

Click to reduce

Points

1 **Intro** level displays menus and palettes such as the Toolbox in the simplest form only. This is useful when you first use PagePlus, because it reduces confusion.

2 At higher levels, the menus and palettes are larger. The illustration shows the Toolbox when **Publisher** or **Professional** level is selected.

3 Even if you work at Intro level, you can see the enhanced Toolbox or Changebar by clicking on the arrowhead, which will then change to a double-arrowhead. Click again to reduce the box size.

Basic steps

1 The **Default Printer** is the one that Windows will normally print to

2 Click on **Specific Printer** if you have other printers installed and want to use one of them. They do not have to be connected, as you can write the output to a file for printing elsewhere.

3 Click on the arrow-head to see the list of installed printers.

4 Pick your printer. **FILE** means that the output is stored in a file. You will be asked for a filename when "print-ing" starts.

The printers that you can use are those that have been set up for Windows - see Windows Made Simple if you are not certain how this is done. When you click the Printer Setup option of the File menu of PagePlus you will see the current settings and you can check what printers have been set up for use with Windows and all programs that use Windows.

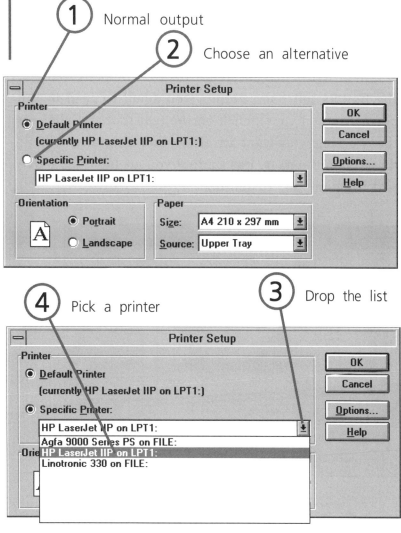

① Normal output

② Choose an alternative

③ Drop the list

④ Pick a printer

Tip

If you create PostScript files, always store them on the hard drive - they may be too large for a floppy.

Printing a page

If you would like to try out the printing routines, take a standard PagePlus template, such as the Quotation, as an example. This will need a little editing first, to convert dollar signs into pound signs, and to make other references more relevant to UK use, as distinct from US use. For example, sales tax references need changing to references to VAT and so on.

The simplest way of editing the text is to use WritePlus on it. This allows you to carry out actions like changing dollar signs to pound signs, using the Find and Replace action of WritePlus. For items like the company name in the bottom left hand corner (too small to read in the normal screen view), click on the text tool and click on the working you want to alter. You can then edit it directly on the page. Use Undo if you accidentally move text from one box to another

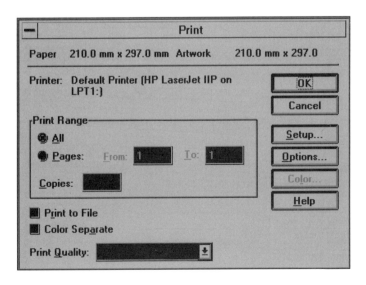

1 Start with the page on screen, ready for printing.

2 Click on **File** and then on **Print**. The Print menu box will appear.

3 Make sure that the **Paper** size you are using is the size noted in the form.

4 Make sure that the **Printer** is as described.

5 Select **All Pages** for this example.

6 Click **OK** to send it to the printer

❑ The **To File** option is used if you do not have the printer named in this box and want to create a file that can be sent to that printer.

❑ The **Options** button is used for more advanced printer setup.

24

Print options

The print options are mainly used when the page size is not the same as the paper size. You can ignore most of these if you have designed for – and are printing on – A4 paper.

Type in a different scale size if you are printing on smaller paper than the page size that you used for designing.

Tiling is used when you want to print a large page on small sheets of paper (like a poster on A4) - the page is printed in sections to be glued together. You can specify the overlap.

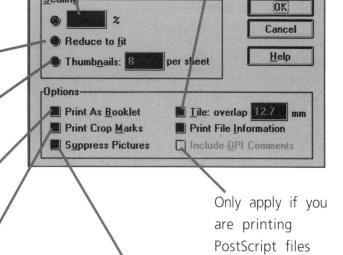

Reduce the page size so that it will fit the paper.

Make miniatures of a set of pages – normally eight to a sheet. Useful if you want an impression of a set of pages.

See Take note panel

Only apply if you are printing PostScript files

Crop marks are used to show where the paper can be cut when the page you have designed is smaller than the paper you print on.

Print frames in place of pictures. Use this for a quick print of a proof, or to allow a photo to be glued in later.

Summary

❑ **Page Size** determines the size of the printed page, and of the margins. This should not be confused with **Sheet Size**, which is the size of the paper.

❑ You can show **crop marks** on the sheet if the page size is smaller than the sheet size

❑ The **General Preferences** box allows you to specify units, and the elements in the display.

❑ The **Ease of Use Preferences** allow you to choose which items in Assistants, Tips and Help to use.

❑ The **Picture Preferences** are set to defaults that you should not change until you have more experience.

❑ **Frame defaults** allow you to specify the frame margin, number of and distance between columns.

❑ Use **Save Settings** to make all of your preferences and defaults more permanent.

❑ You can use the Printer Setup options of the File menu to change printer.

❑ To print, use the **File** menu and the **Print** option.

❑ For a simple page, use the default settings of **All pages**, otherwise you can specify a range of pages.

❑ You can opt to print to a file if you want to use a printer that is not connected to your computer.

❑ The **print options** deal with special requirements.

❑ The option for creating **booklets** allows printing to be done on larger sheets which can then be folded and stapled. The folded paper will then show the pages in their correct numbered order.

4 Working with text

Using type

The characters of text are not of one standard design. A set of letter and number symbols of one design constitutes a typeface, and the number of typefaces available to you is vast - more than you will ever need.

Typeface designs can be divided into book, sans-serif, and display. Display typefaces are used for advertising fliers and other short-text work, with sans-serif used for less ostentatious text. Book typefaces must be easy to read when the amount of text is large.

Each typeface design is known by name, such a Times New Roman, Arial, or Frankenstein (the examples used here). For each typeface, you can use different character sizes, and different styles (fonts or founts)

This is a book typeface

This is a sans-serif typeface

This is a display typeface

Tip

Aim to always use Truetype fonts - other fonts will not print as they look on the screen.

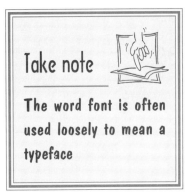

Take note

The word font is often used loosely to mean a typeface

Classes of typeface

❑ A **book** typeface is one that should not be tiring to read when you need to read a lot of it. This example is Times New Roman.

This

Technically this is a serif face - each limb of a letter ends in a small hook or pair of hooks, the serifs.

❑ A **sans-serif** typeface looks very plain.

This

Though it can be used for text it is normally reserved for small pieces of text such as captions.

❑ A **display** typeface demands attention and is used for headings, particularly in advertising material. It is very tiring to read if used for a large amount of text.

Basic steps

1 Select the word(s) you want to emphasise by dragging the cursor across with the mouse button held down.

2 Open the **Text** menu and select **Font Style**.

3 Click on the style you want.

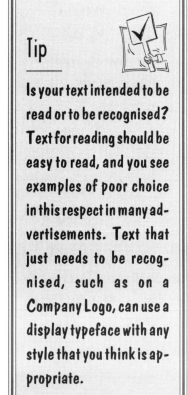

Tip

Is your text intended to be read or to be recognised? Text for reading should be easy to read, and you see examples of poor choice in this respect in many advertisements. Text that just needs to be recognised, such as on a Company Logo, can use a display typeface with any style that you think is appropriate.

Typestyles or fonts are variations on the characters of a typeface. For example, bold type is thicker and more spaced out than the normal (regular or Roman), and Italic type is slanted and thinner. Some typefaces offer bold italic, and a few offer effects like outline, underline and strikethrough. These last three should be used only if the effect they produce justifies their appearance.

Use normal, regular, or Roman style for most of your text.

Use **bold** for **headings** or to **emphasise** a word or phrase.

Italic is another way of emphasising, often used in place of *quotemarks*, or for *picture captions*.

Bold Italic can be used, but is ***not*** common.

Underline , strikethrough and other florid effects should seldom be used because they are tiring to read.

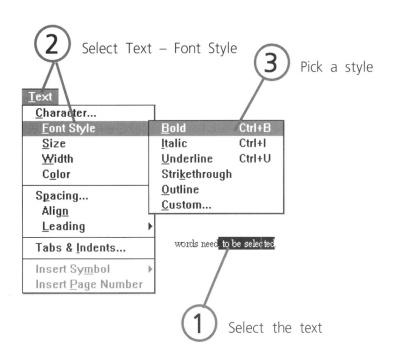

② Select Text – Font Style

③ Pick a style

① Select the text

Type sizes

The size of type is the height of its CAPITAL letters. All capitals are of the same height, but the widths vary considerably, depending on the width of the letter itself and the design and style. This is why the width of a phrase will change as you change its typeface and font style.

Most typefaces are **proportionally spaced**, meaning that characters such as **m** take up more width than characters like **i**. Typewriters use monospacing with each character of the same overall width. You can imitate typewriter text by using a *Courier* typeface.

Size can range from ₄ₚₒᵢₙₜ to **72**

This uses a proportionally-spaced face

This uses Courier, a monospaced face.

Special Units

A **point** is 1/72 of an inch. For example, 12-point lettering is 1/6 inch high. *Work in points unless you have some compelling reason to use other units.*

The **pica** is equal to 12 point, or 1/6 inch.

The **cicero** is a Continental unit equal to 5/11 cm (and you thought they would use exact metric units?).

The **didot** is another Continental unit, approximately 0.378 mm high.

Choices

1 **Left-aligned text** is like typed work and can be easier to read than badly-spaced justified text. The text aligns to the left with a ragged right edge.

2 **Fully-justified text** looks best on wide lines. It takes the full width of the frame unless the lines are short.

3 **Centre alignment** is useful for headings and in fliers where there are only a few lines of text. The text is centred between the boundaries.

4 **Right-aligned text** is used for addresses on letter sheets. Text is set to the right with a ragged left edge.

Text is placed between margins, which might be the page margins or the margins imposed by a frame (which need not be the same). Within these boundaries you can lay out text in four different ways.

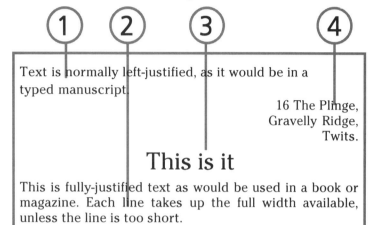

Text is normally left-justified, as it would be in a typed manuscript.

16 The Plinge,
Gravelly Ridge,
Twits.

This is it

This is fully-justified text as would be used in a book or magazine. Each line takes up the full width available, unless the line is too short.

Take note

If you want to set all of your work using full-justification, click in succession on **Tools - Defaults - Text - Selected values - Spacing - Justify**. You can alter the alignment of any selected text (drag the cursor over the text) by using the **Text** menu, and selecting **Align**.

Tip

Do not worry too much about the alignment when you start work on a publication. It is easy to alter its alignment, so that you can experiment to find out what looks best for your pages.

Spacing text

Spaces are an important feature of text. There are spaces between characters, spaces between words, and spaces between lines. All of these have a considerable effect on the way words look in print.

Alterations to tracking cannot be made while you are using PagePlus in Intro level - you need to switch to Professional level to find the **Tracking** option in the **Text** menu. You select tracking from a list that ranges from *very loose* to *very tight*, with a **Custom** option also.

Word spacing is changed by clicking on the **Text** menu, and selecting **Spacing** and then **Advanced**. You are asked to fill in percentage amounts for minimum, optimum and maximum spacing, and spacing on the last (unjustified) line of a set of justified lines.

Leading is changed from the **Text** menu, clicking on the **Leading** option and selecting the percentage. The default is 120%

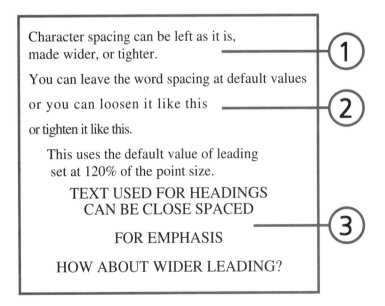

Character spacing can be left as it is, made wider, or tighter.

You can leave the word spacing at default values

or you can loosen it like this

or tighten it like this.

This uses the default value of leading set at 120% of the point size.

TEXT USED FOR HEADINGS CAN BE CLOSE SPACED

FOR EMPHASIS

HOW ABOUT WIDER LEADING?

1 **Tracking** controls the space between characters. Wide spacing (loose tracking) looks untidy, close spacing (tight tracking) can be difficult to read.

2 **Word spacing** should not be altered unless you are sure that it will improve the text. Reducing spacing allows you to cram in more text, but readability can suffer

3 Spacing between lines (**leading**, pronounced 'ledding') is usually 120% of point size of lettering, so that 10-point lettering would use 12-point leading.

Tip

If you have no strong views on the subject, leave the defaults as they are.

1 Paragraph spacing is, by default, 0%, meaning that no extra spacing is put after paragraphs as compared to the spacing between lines.

2 You can also opt for an extra **space above** a paragraph.

3 **Kerning** refers to closing the character spacing between certain pairs of letters (like A and W). This is needed only for larger sizes of type (above 16 points), and you can opt here for the size above which kerning will be done automatically.

Paragraph spacing in PagePlus is altered by using the **Spacing** options from the **Text** menu. This is available at all levels of PagePlus. The spacing options include alignment and character spacing as well as the Advanced options that can be used to control word spacing.

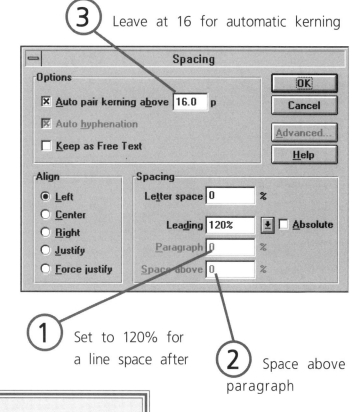

③ Leave at 16 for automatic kerning

① Set to 120% for a line space after

② Space above paragraph

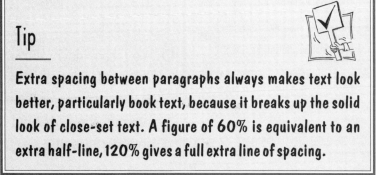

Tip

Extra spacing between paragraphs always makes text look better, particularly book text, because it breaks up the solid look of close-set text. A figure of 60% is equivalent to an extra half-line, 120% gives a full extra line of spacing.

Indents

If PagePlus is to be used to create eye-catching layouts, its ability to handle special text effects is critical. This section is devoted to the most important of these effects. A common text trick is to make the first line of each paragraph indented, meaning that it is further away from the left margin of the page. A variation on this is a hanging indent, with the first line starting nearer the margin.

First line   Left   Right   ④   Click OK

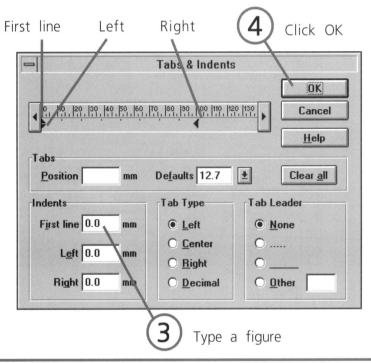

③ Type a figure

Here is a text in which the first word of each paragraph has been indented positively, so that the space between the first word and the margin is greater than for the other lines in the paragraph.

The use of indenting is a useful way of drawing attention to a new paragraph.

Now we can look at the effect of a hanging indent, with the first line indented to the left
    and the remainder of the paragraph indented to the right.
You can specify a negative distance for the first line indent, and use a positive (left) indent
    for the lines other than the first.

Sometimes, you want to make a paragraph stand out from the others in a way that shows it is a quotation or some special explanation, for example.

    You can do this by indenting both sides of the paragraph, leaving the first
    line indent at zero, and specifying an indent distance for both left and right
    – in this example 10 mm.

Basic steps

1 Select the text.

2 Click on the **Text** menu and then on **Tabs and Indents**.

3 At the **Tabs and Indents** dialog box, type in a figure for **First line indent**.

4 Click on **OK**.

❑ You will see the first lines indented. Look at the **Tabs and Indents** dialog box again and you will see the marker that indicates a first-line indent.

5 To make a hanging indent set a **left indent** and an equal *negative* **first line indent** - in this example, the left indent is 10 mm and the first line indent is - 10 mm.

6 You can indent both **left** and **right** to make a paragraph stand out among the surrounding paragraphs.

Basic steps

1 To make a dropped capital, remove the normal capital from the framed paragraph, using **[Delete]**.

2 Using free text, make a capital in the pasteboard, and format it to the size and face you want to use.

3 Switch to the arrow tool. A wide frame will appear.

4 Shrink the frame around the capital letter.

5 Use **Tools – Wrap** to open the **Wrap Settings** dialog box and specify **Wrap Outside**.

6 Place the cursor on the *paragraph* and open the **Wrap Settings** dialog box - specify **Text will Wrap**.

7 Position the capital and watch the text wrap around it.

This will use a dropped capital

Another way of drawing the reader's eye to the text is to emphasise the first capital letter of a paragraph. One simple way of doing this is to make it **bold**, or to use a display font, such as *Frankenstein*, for that letter alone.

Even better is to use a dropped or raised capital. This involves using some graphics effects, but it can all be done using Intro level. The paragraph must be in a frame.

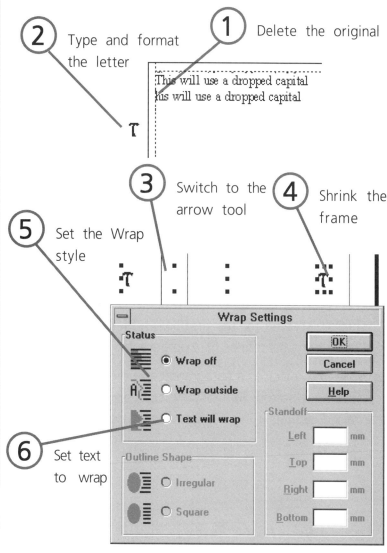

② Type and format the letter

① Delete the original

This will use a dropped capital
his will use a dropped capital

③ Switch to the arrow tool

④ Shrink the frame

⑤ Set the Wrap style

⑥ Set text to wrap

Wrap Settings

Status
- ● Wrap off
- ○ Wrap outside
- ○ Text will wrap

OK
Cancel
Help

Standoff
- Left [ ] mm
- Top [ ] mm
- Right [ ] mm
- Bottom [ ] mm

Outline Shape
- ○ Irregular
- ○ Square

Summary

- The **typeface** is the design of the letters, numerals and punctuation marks that make up a set. Each typeface is named.

- Typefaces can be classed as **book**, **sans-serif**, and **display**.

- Each typeface will contain **styles** or **fonts** to emphasise words. Apart from normal, there are bold and italic, with more exotic styles in some faces.

- The **size** of a typeface is expressed in points. **Spacings** are often expressed as percentages of this value.

- For special effects, you can alter the spacing between characters, words and lines (leading).

- You can also alter the **space between paragraphs**. An increased space can makes large amounts of text look less intimidating.

- **Kerning** means decreasing the spacing between certain pairs of letters, and this will be done automatically on text that is above the designated point size (16 points by default).

- PagePlus can produce **indented** text, by setting the margin spacing for the first line, all left-hand lines, or all right-hand lines of a paragraph.

- The first letter of a paragraph can be emphasised by making it bold or in a display font, or dropped or a raised capital, using a larger size of typeface.

5 Frames

Using frames

Frames are an essential part of working with PagePlus, as with many DTP programs. They offer a way to control the layout of a page, and are like independent pages, capable of holding text or graphics, and with their own margins and columns. The important difference is that you can move them and alter their size and shape as you please. Let's look at how we can prepare more than one frame on a page and run text in so that it fills all of the frames.

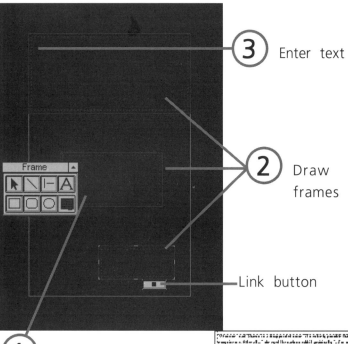

③ Enter text

② Draw frames

Link button

① Use the frame tool

④ Text flows from one to the next

Basic steps

1 Select the frame tool

2 Draw out the frames on the page.

❏ Each frame has a small 'link button' at its bottom right-hand corner.

3 Click on the text tool **A** and place the cursor in the top frame. You can type text, use WritePlus, or import text.

4 The text automatically flows into each frame in turn. Any surplus is stored until you create more frames.

Tip

If you import a large amount of text into a page, more frames will be created automatically on new pages as required.

Points

1 If you have created a frame, creating a second directly afterwards will ensure that the frames are linked.

2 The **Frame Link** button allows you to control how frames are linked.

3 When frames are linked, clicking on the link button will unlink them, and the square dot will turn blue. The cursor also changes shape. If the frames were not linked, clicking on the link button will link them.

Linking means that text imported or typed into a frame will automatically overflow into the next frame. If frames are not linked, then overflow text is held in memory and can be used when a frame is ready for it. If you switch off with text suspended in this way you will lose the text.

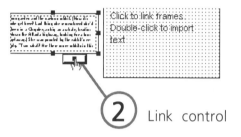

② Link control

As you move the cursor away from the link button, the broken link cursor ▢▯ appears. You can then:

❑ click on any empty piece of page or pasteboard to break the link

❑ click on an empty frame, to link that frame to the one whose link you broke.

❑ click on the same frame, to clear it, and use it as the first frame of a new text "story".

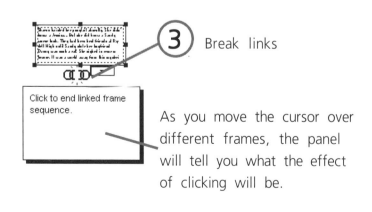

③ Break links

As you move the cursor over different frames, the panel will tell you what the effect of clicking will be.

Take note

In **PagePlus**, a story means a set of paragraphs that belong together. The story might be spread across several frames, as it often is in a newspaper.

Frames within frames

You can place one frame inside another. This is usually applied to put pictures inside text, but you can equally well place text inside text. In this sense, 'inside' means that the inner text is contained in its own frame, not covered by the outside text, as illustrated here.

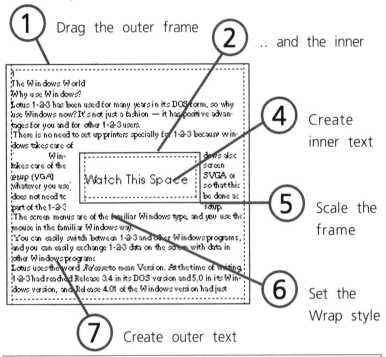

① Drag the outer frame

② .. and the inner

④ Create inner text

Watch This Space

⑤ Scale the frame

⑥ Set the Wrap style

⑦ Create outer text

1 Select the frame tool 🖼 and drag out the outer frame.

2 Drag out the inner frame.

3 Break the link between the frames.

4 Select the text tool **A**, and type the text for the inner frame. Select the text and apply a larger face.

5 Select the pointer tool ▸, and scale the inner frame to fit the text size.

6 Select the inner frame, and use the **Tools** menu to choose **Wrap Settings** of **Wrap Outside** and **Square**.

7 Select the text tool, place the cursor in the outer frame, and import or type text

Tip

Watch the cursor shape and Quickhelp messages when you are selecting. With the cursor in the inner frame, the message refers to the text object. With the cursor just outside the edge of the frame, the message refers to the frame object. Select the frame object for linking and wrapping, the text object for making changes (bold, italic) to text.

40

Basic steps

1 Select the pointer tool and click on the block so that handles appear

2 Place the cursor on the block and hold the button down until the cursor changes shape

3 Drag the mouse, with the button held down, until the text block is where you want it.

Whether you use a frame or not, each paragraph of a piece of text can be selected with the pointer as if it were a unit. This unit is called a text block, and when you click on a paragraph you will see the familiar square "handles" appear. These allow you to use the pointer tool to move and alter the shape and size of the text block.

The cursor above appears if a frame has been drawn and text put into it. The ⊕ cursor appears on freetext and on selected frames – as distinct from text inside the frame.

Take note

The shape of the cursor depends upon whether you type freetext or type text into a frame.

Tip

Do not worry too much about the size or shape of a frame when you first create it. Knowing how you want to use it is more important, because you can alter the size and shape later.

Summary

❑   Frames are essential to PagePlus. They can be linked to provide continuity of text.

❑   The control of linking is achieved by the use of the link button.

❑   When you move a frame, its text moves with it.

❑   When you alter the size of a frame, the text will adjust to the new size - if any text disappears it can be linked in to another frame.

❑   The frame contains its own margins to ensure that its contents do not become placed hard against the contents in another frame.

6   Adding pictures

Inserting pictures

PagePlus deals with objects. A block of text is an object, and a picture is another object. The reason for using the name is to emphasise that the actions that you can carry out on a picture are much the same as you can carry out on a text block - you can place it in a frame or leave it free, move it, resize it, or reshape it by dragging the frame handles. Inserting a picture into text follows much the same lines as inserting a piece of text into text.

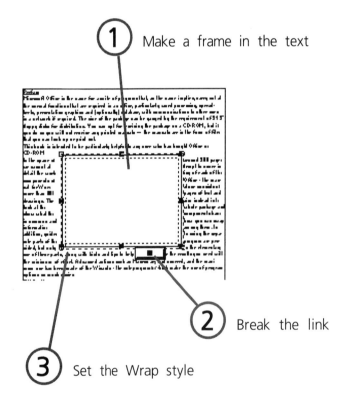

① Make a frame in the text

② Break the link

③ Set the Wrap style

Take note

You can import the picture without using a frame, as it will use a frame of its own.

44

8 Choose an image and click the **OK** button.

9 Drag out a space for the picture. The cursor changes shape and the picture is inserted.

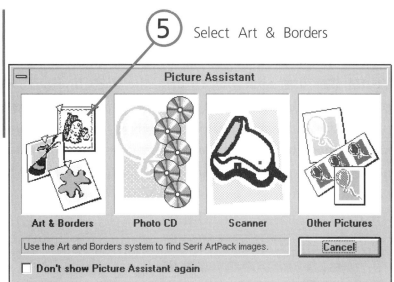

(5) Select Art & Borders

(6) Select Art

(8) Choose and OK

(9) Drag a shape

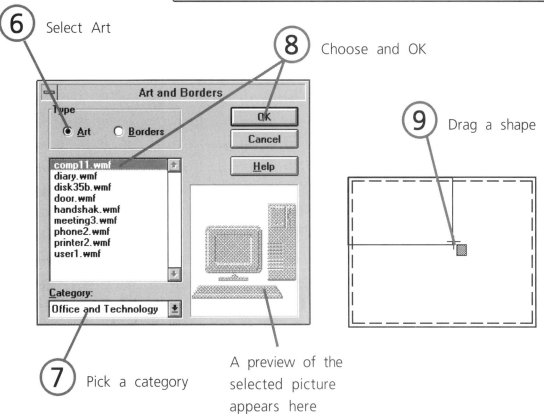

(7) Pick a category

A preview of the selected picture appears here

Picture types

PagePlus can work with three types of pictures. The simplest type is the bitmap, which uses a file that describes the position and colour of each dot in a picture. Vector files use equations to describe each line in the picture. OLE objects are items created by other Windows programs. They can be pictures, tables, text, or even sounds, and they can be embedded in a page (permanently in place) or linked (meaning that the file is held separately and not as part of the page).

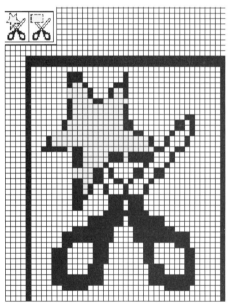

In bitmaps, each pixel can be edited for fine adjustment

Vector graphics scale well, but are harder to edit

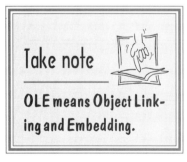

Take note

OLE means Object Linking and Embedding.

❏ **Bitmaps** files are created using Paintbrush and other paint packages. The advantage of a bitmap is that you can edit each bit. The disadvantage is that a bitmap looks best at the size it had when created – it does not scale well.

❏ **Vector** files are created by CAD and drawing programs, including Serif's DrawPlus. They cannot be edited so easily, but they scale well, remaining clear at any size.

❏ **OLE** images can be bitmap or vector. Double-clicking on an OLE image allows you to edit it, using the program that created it. If the OLE is **linked**, it does not add to the size of the PagePlus file. If it is **embedded**, it is stored in the PagePlus file.

46

Rules

1 If the picture can be inserted at its original size PagePlus will do so. When you have selected your image, click on the page or pasteboard to import it at its original size.

2 If a **bitmap** picture cannot be inserted at original size, PagePlus will use a size that will print clearly.

3 If a **vector** picture cannot be inserted at original size, PagePlus will use a default size.

4 The **width** that will be used is indicated by the white area on the ruler line

Picture size is a problem that can cause some headaches until you have acquired some experience. When you scale a bitmap, you are either reducing the number of dots or increasing them, and the only alternative for scaling up is to use larger dots. When you scale a vector picture it will look better at simple multiples (like 1.5 or 0.75) than at complex multiples like 0.783.

PagePlus follows a set of rules, opposite, concerning picture scaling.

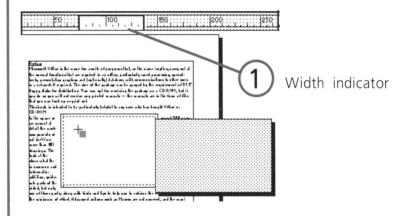

Width indicator

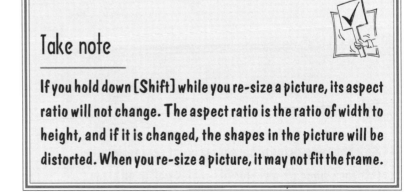

Take note

If you hold down [Shift] while you re-size a picture, its aspect ratio will not change. The aspect ratio is the ratio of width to height, and if it is changed, the shapes in the picture will be distorted. When you re-size a picture, it may not fit the frame.

Resizing pictures

The **[Ctrl]** key can be used when you re-size a bitmap or vector picture. The effect in each case is to avoid re-sizing ratios which have a poor appearance when printed, and you will not necessarily see any effect on the screen. In addition, not all types of vector picture will respond to this action, and in some examples, the sizes that are best for printing may simply not be suitable.

For example, if the *BUS.WMF* file that is part of the Arts & Borders set is put onto a page, you will find that the smallest optimum size almost fills the page, and the next size up is much too wide.

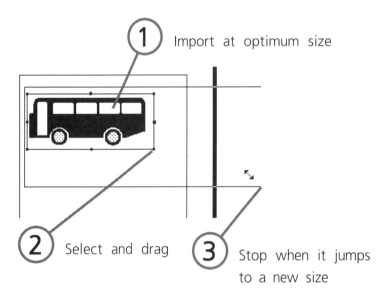

(1) Import at optimum size

(2) Select and drag

(3) Stop when it jumps to a new size

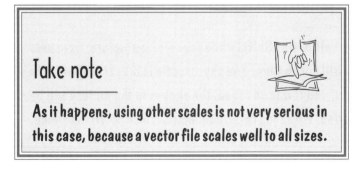

Take note

As it happens, using other scales is not very serious in this case, because a vector file scales well to all sizes.

1 Import the picture with the **File – Import Picture** option. Click on the page to place the picture at its optimum size.

2 Click to reveal the handles if they are not visible. Click on a corner handle, and when the cursor changes shape, hold down **[Ctrl]**.

3 Drag out the box shape that appears until it suddenly jumps to a larger size.

4 Release the mouse button to see the picture at the new size.

5 If you try to repeat this to find a size smaller than the imported size you will find that there is no suitable smaller size.

Basic steps

1 Import the bitmap file in the usual way and click on the page to place it at its original size.

❑ In this example, the original size is too large for the page, and will need to be reduced.

2 Click on a corner handle and when the cursor changes shape, press **[Ctrl]** down and drag the box size down to the minimum that can be used.

3 Release the mouse button to see the picture at this magnification.

Tip

You can often get a reasonable idea of how such a file will look in print by looking at it on screen at a higher magnification.

Bitmap pictures

The use of **[Ctrl]** when re-sizing a picture applies also to bitmap types, and it is particularly important when the picture contains pattern fills. At some magnifications, such patterns either disappear or become uneven, and the resulting printed page looks very poor.

You have to see the printed page to be sure, because a bitmap picture that looks poor on a standard VGA screen (75 dots per inch) often looks quite acceptable when printed with the usual 300 dots per inch of a laser printer.

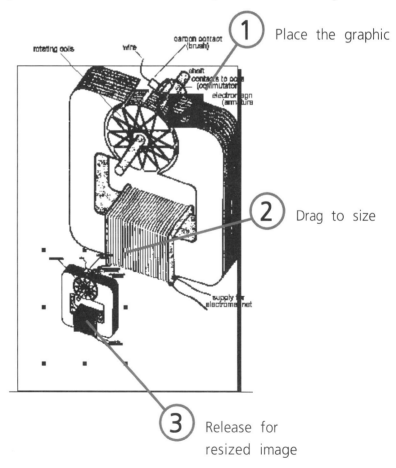

① Place the graphic

② Drag to size

③ Release for resized image

Pix tricks

There are several changes that can be made to an imported picture. These apply also to other objects, but are more frequently used with pictures.

- All of these effects can be achieved by using a menu and some can also be achieved by using the tools.

- Where you have a choice, only the **Tools** options will be illustrated here.

Flip vertical

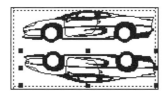

Flip horizontal

Double flip

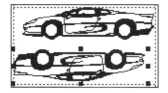

Effects

1 **Flip** reverses a picture, as if in a mirror. Use the **Tools** menu to change to **Publisher** or **Professional** level, then select the picture and use the **Graphics – Flip** option. You can flip either horizontally or vertically – or both!

Take note

The Windows **Cut** and **Paste** facilities are used here as normal.

You can select an image and then use **Cut** or **Copy** from the **Edit** menu.

A **Cut** or **Copied** image can be pasted in using **Edit – Paste**, at any place you click the cursor.

2 Rotate. Select the image, click on the **Rotate** tool 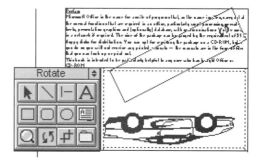 (Publisher or Professional level) and click on one of the object handles, then drag to rotate.

3 **Crop** reduces the displayed size of an image by using the **Crop** tool on a selected image – click on a handle and drag.

- Remember that a rotated image can look very ragged – check how it will appear on paper before you fix it in place.
- Almost every picture can be improved by cropping to remove un-needed background. Many illustrations look much clearer in black and white.

Rotate

Crop

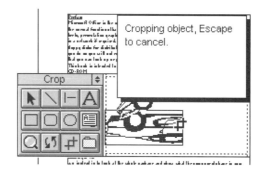

Tip

You can use Copy and Paste to make a copy of an image, and then use actions like flip or rotate as a way of creating multiple images

Picture Preferences

The Picture Preferences are obtained from the Tools menu by way of the Preferences section, and though the default settings are suitable for most purposes you might after some experience want to make changes.

Remember that an embedded picture adds to the size of the page file, so that linking is better if your pictures are large and detailed. The drawback is that the picture file has to be loaded in each time the page is displayed. In general, all of these options are concerned with the trade-off between file size and the speed with which you can change from one page to another on screen.

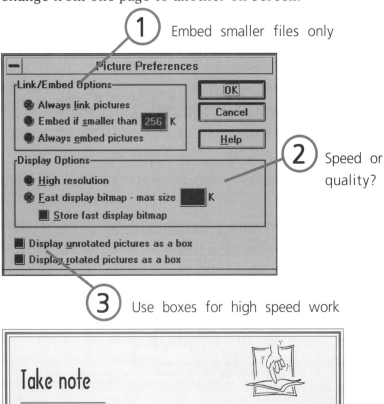

Embed smaller files only

Speed or quality?

Use boxes for high speed work

Take note

If you work with PostScript files, these will always be large no matter how you opt to treat picture files.

Options

1 The **Always Link** option keeps the publication file small, as the picture data is held in the separate files. With **Always Embed**, the data is duplicated. **Embed if smaller than** ... is a useful compromise. Use a value fo 64k, rather than 256k, for smaller ppp files.

2 Use **High Resolution** only if you need it, because it slows down your work on a page. **Fast display bitmap** displays pictures in lower detail, but at high speed. Store fast display bitmap allows for faster display when files are opened, but the files are larger.

3 The **box** options make the display of pictures very much faster, but the detail of the pictures are not visible. A good compromise is to display only **rotated pictures** as a box.

The Toolbox

The illustration shows the Toolbox as it appears in Publisher or Professional level, or when the arrowhead has been clicked to expand the Toolbar.

The illustration also shows the Import Picture symbol with its explanation appearing in QuickHelp - the other symbols are explained, left.

The pointer, used to work with frames and text-blocks.

The text tool, used to place and select text.

Five tools for drawing shapes — straight line, line at 0°, 45° and 90°, box, rounded box and oval (or circle). See page 86

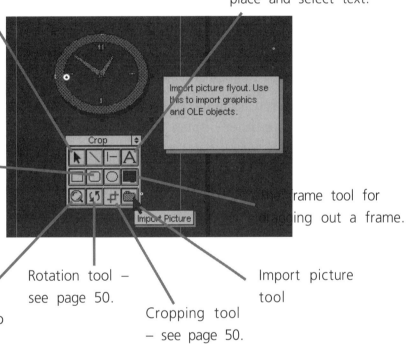

The frame tool for dragging out a frame.

Rotation tool — see page 50.

Cropping tool — see page 50.

Import picture tool

Zoom tool to allow you to increase or decrease the scale of the screen view of the page. You can click this symbol and then drag the page size. Hold down [Shift] to make the page view smaller.

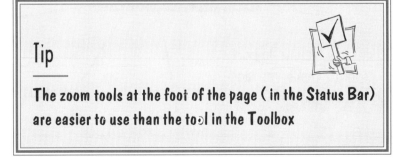

Tip

The zoom tools at the foot of the page (in the Status Bar) are easier to use than the tool in the Toolbox

Toolbox changes

When you work in Publisher or Professional level, or if you click the arrowhead on the Toolbox, you will see an extended Toolbox. The items of the Toolbox have been noted earlier, but one point that was omitted then was the effect of clicking on the **Picture Import** icon.

When you click this icon, another set of tools appears, of which several have no action unless you have installed PagePlus add-on programs.

● TypePlus is used for creating typographical effects, such as making text wrap around a cylinder.

● TablePlus is used to generate spreadsheet displays.

● PhotoPlus is used as a bitmap editor for scanned photographs and other bitmap images.

● DrawPlus is a high-grade vector drawing program. These programs work along with PagePlus and are sold separately.

Tip

Watch out for special offers on these add-on programs

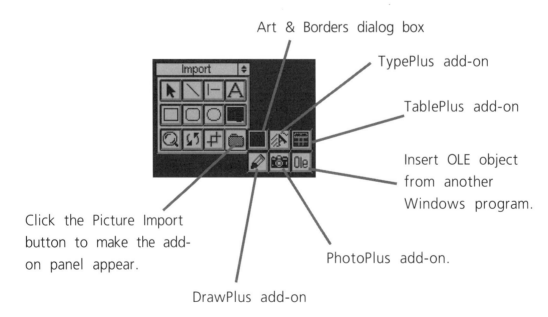

Art & Borders dialog box

TypePlus add-on

TablePlus add-on

Insert OLE object from another Windows program.

Click the Picture Import button to make the add-on panel appear.

PhotoPlus add-on.

DrawPlus add-on

The Changebar

We have looked at several of the facilities that the Toolbox offers, but we have so far completely ignored the **Changebar**, which is a way of changing the properties of objects. Let's see what it has to offer.

This Changebar relates to the picture, and has been expanded by clicking the arrowhead

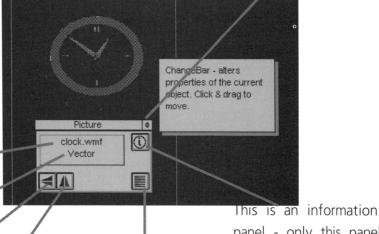

Name of the file

Type of graphics file, vector in this case.

Flip the picture vertically

Flip the picture horizontally

Wrap or position (front or back) controls (Publisher or Professional level only)

This is an information panel - only this panel is visible at Intro level.

Summary

❏ You can **insert a picture** into a frame or any part of a page, either over text or with text wrapped around it.

❏ The pictures that come with PagePlus are in the **Arts & Borders** directory, and are grouped by theme.

❏ When **importing a picture**, click to import it at its original size; drag, and it will fill the dragged space.

❏ PagePlus can work with **bitmap** or **vector** pictures.

❏ An **embedded** picture is saved with the page file. A **linked** picture is held separately, so the page file is smaller. Either can be edited by double-clicking on it.

❏ **Vector** files will scale without loss of detail. **Bitmap** files can be edited by changing bits and can present a very poor appearance when magnified.

❏ Use **[Shift]** or **[Ctrl]**, while dragging a picture frame, to keep the aspect ratio, or drag to a preferred size.

❏ Pictures and other objects can be **flipped** (mirrored), **rotated** through any angle, and **cropped** to show only a portion of the whole picture.

❏ The **Picture Preferences** dialog box allows you to determine your own options for resolution and speed of use. If you have a slow machine you might want to use all the options that made for faster use.

❏ The **Changebar** offers information on pictures, and, when expanded, allows you to flip pictures and control wrapping and layering.

❏ The extended **Toolbox** contains tools that can be used on pictures and other objects. Click the **Picture Import** icon to see a list of sources, some of which are available only if you have the add-on programs.

7 Layout tools

Rulers

The Rulers of PagePlus are the graduated strips that run across the top of the page display and down the left hand side.

The numbering of the rulers will use the units that you have fixed using the Tools menu and clicking on Preferences and General. The example shows the use of millimetre units for an A4 page size.

The ruler units are always shown at the same scale as the page, so that any measurements that you make using a zoomed view will still be correct on any other view scale.

The point where each ruler has its zero is the origin or zero-point. You can move this point by clicking and dragging the zero-point icon. This allows you to drag either or both rulers to a new point. The default position is at the top left hand corner of the pasteboard, and for some work you might want to drag the zero point to the top left hand corner of your page, or to the top left hand corner of the text area (where the margins meet).

Take note

You can return the zero point of the rulers after it has been moved. Simply double-click on the zero-point icon.

You can move the rulers but keep the zero point at its original position if you drag the rulers with [Shift] held down.

If you find that the zero mark on one or both rulers is not at the intersection, click once on the zero-point icon.

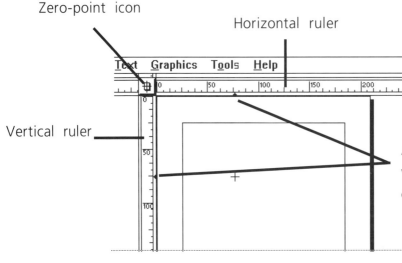

Zero-point icon

Horizontal ruler

Vertical ruler

Arrowheads marking the vertical and horizontal cursor positions

Using the rulers

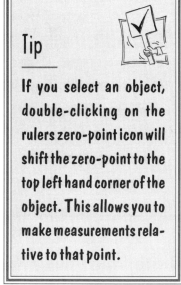

Tip

If you select an object, double-clicking on the rulers zero-point icon will shift the zero-point to the top left hand corner of the object. This allows you to make measurements relative to that point.

The rulers come into their own when you are trying to position objects (blocks of text or pictures) on a page. By using the rulers along with *snapping* (see later) you can ensure that an object is positioned exactly where you want it, even if your mouse-movements are not as precise as you would like.

You should always work with rulers displayed. The only time you need to switch them off is when you are finally reviewing pages and you want to see what the text and pictures look like with no other display on the screen.

When you select any object on the page, the rulers will show highlighted areas which pinpoint the position and size of the object

Layout Tools dialog box

Open this by clicking on **Page** and then **Layout**. Each box can be clicked to turn its effect on or off. Page guides and Snapping are dealt with in the following pages.

Lock rulers so they cannot be moved

Lock page guides

Ruler display on or off

Page guides on or off

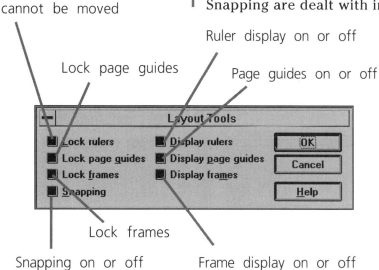

Snapping on or off

Lock frames

Frame display on or off

Tip

When you move rulers or other guides, it's always wise to lock them in place to avoid accidental movement when you are clicking the mouse button on other objects.

Using snaps

If you have tried moving the zero-point of the rulers to the edge of the page you will have noticed how easy it was to get the rulers exactly positioned. This is because of the use of **Snaps**. Snapping means that you only have to get one object (the rulers in this case) close enough to another (the page corner), and the two will snap together. Using Snaps, there is never any "almost there" - you have either positioned objects perfectly, or nowhere near each other.

You cannot alter the snap distance, but the list of snap points, right, shows that you can snap to anything useful. In particular, you can always snap to a page margin, a ruler point, a guide (see later), and a frame margin.

Tip

Always work with Snaps on as far as possible as this makes it much easier to ensure that objects on the page are aligned.

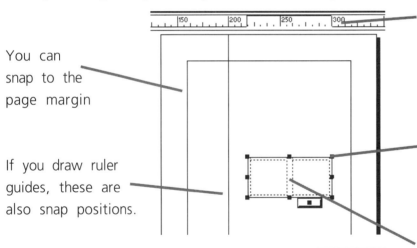

You can snap to the page margin

If you draw ruler guides, these are also snap positions.

The default snap points are the markings (increments) on the ruler

You can snap to the frame margins

You can snap to column guides in a frame.

Tip

Turn snapping on and off in the Layout Tools dialog box (See page 59). You might want to turn it off when trying to align an object such as a circle so that its rim touched another object.

Using guides

1 Create a guide by clicking on the ruler line. Clicking on the *horizontal* ruler will create a **vertical** guide; clicking on the *vertical* ruler will create a **horizontal** guide line.

❏ The guide position will snap to a ruler marking unless you have turned **Snapping** off.

2 **Move** a guide to any point on the page by dragging

3 **Remove** a guide by dragging it right off the page.

4 Use a guide to align objects if they have to be placed at a distance from the margin.

5 You can use guides to show how large a frame needs to be.

A guide is a line that is drawn to help you align objects on the page. Unlike a margin, a guide is not a fixed part of the page and does not correspond to any part of the page.

Guides appear on the screen (coloured red), but do not appear on the printed page. You can turn the guides on or off using the **Page - Display** options, or the **Page - Layout Tools** dialog box.

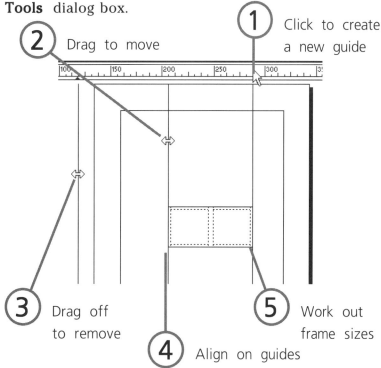

① Click to create a new guide
② Drag to move
③ Drag off to remove
④ Align on guides
⑤ Work out frame sizes

Take note

If your work is concerned mainly with text you might not need to make use of guides. They are particularly useful, however, when you have to line up text and illustrations on a page as they make the task much easier if you work with Snapping on.

Status bar

The Status bar is the strip at the bottom of the PagePlus display. This contains a mixture of text and icons that provide both information and control actions. The Status bar exists in three versions, one for each level of PagePlus.

Intro

The Intro level status bar, illustrated on this page, is the simplest, and it contains the information and commands that you are likely to make most use of.

Using this bar you can invoke WritePlus, control the zoom level, check position and size of a text block, and change the level of use between Intro, Publisher, and Professional.

Tip

Discipline yourself to keep glancing at the Status Bar as you work on a page. The information is useful, particularly when you are using higher levels, and many of the actions that you need are available from this bar.

Open WritePlus, the built-in word-processor

Return to a single page view

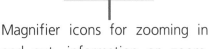

Magnifier icons for zooming in and out, information on zoom level, and the 1:1 zoom icon

The information box contains data about the position and size of a selected block of text

The level icon shows the three levels of PagePlus, with the one in use shaded.

Take note

You can conceal the Status Bar by using the Tools menu, clicking on Preferences and General

Higher level status bars

The status bars for the higher levels of Publisher and Professional contain more information and icons. The extra parts of the higher level status bars are shown here.

Publisher level

The extra items are mainly concerned with moving between pages.

Forward one page

Back one page

Show or hide ruler display

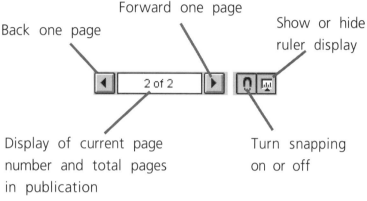

Display of current page number and total pages in publication

Turn snapping on or off

Professional level

The extra items are mainly concerned with controlling what guides and tools are displayed on the screen.

Show or hide Changebar.

Show or hide toolbox.

Edit position, size, rotation

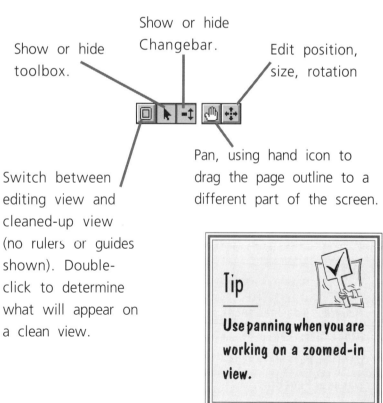

Switch between editing view and cleaned-up view (no rulers or guides shown). Double-click to determine what will appear on a clean view.

Pan, using hand icon to drag the page outline to a different part of the screen.

Tip

Use panning when you are working on a zoomed-in view.

Changing properties

Properties (like text font, colour and so on) can be changed by using menus, but the **Changebar** offers a faster and often more convenient method of making such changes. The changes are obtained by clicking on the Property button, but there will be no effect unless you are working at Publisher or Professional level. You will be reminded of this by a Tip window appearing, unless you have opted not to see the Tips. The Pullout box has been blown apart in this view, and the icons are the ones that apply to text.

1 Click on a property icon

2 Use the slider control or the drop down list in the Changebar to change the property - the font size property is being changed in this example.

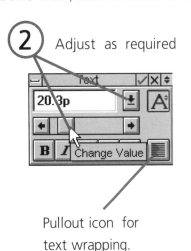

② Adjust as required ① Click on icon

Pullout icon for text wrapping.

Take note

When an unfamiliar icon appears, you can place the cursor over it and look for the QuickHelp note.

Tip

A style is a defined set of properties. Leave these until you have more experience of PagePlus.

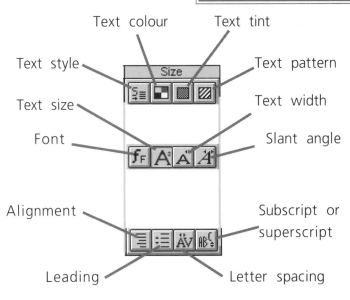

Text colour   Text tint

Text style   Text pattern

Text size   Text width

Font   Slant angle

Alignment   Subscript or superscript

Leading   Letter spacing

Other Changebars

Changebar for a selected picture

Changebar for a selected frame

The way that the Changebar can be used differs according to what you have selected. This page focuses on the main pullout for graphics selected. *Graphics* in this case means drawings created by PagePlus or DrawPlus. The range of pullout icons that is available will depend on what the drawing shape is (line, circle, or box). For example, the icon for rounding the corners of a box will not be present if the shape is not a box.

There are other Changebars for other selected objects, such as picture and frame, and a form of Changebar which appears when no object has been selected.

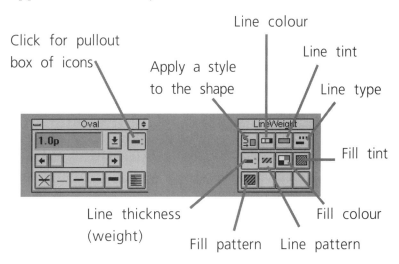

Changebar when no object is selected

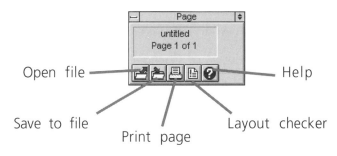

Take note

When a Changebar refers to a frame, you can use the buttons to select the number of columns (one to three), and you can click an information button to find the position of the frame relative to text, along with the filename of a frame's story.

Summary

- **Rulers** assist you with positioning and measuring.

- You can **turn the ruler display on or off,** and move the rulers by dragging the zero-point icon.

- If you **drag the rulers** with [Shift] held down, the zero point will remain fixed.

- You can **lock the positions** of rulers and guides.

- The **snap** action ensures that when you position an object it will line up with snap points.

- Snapping will be to margins, ruler graduations, guides, frame margins and column margins.

- You can draw and move guides as an aid to positioning and sizing objects on the page.

- A guide can be removed by dragging it off the page.

- The **Status Bar** contains useful information and, depending on the level of use of PagePlus, several icons that provide short-cuts to menu actions.

- At **Professional** level, there is a **Pan** button which allows you to move a image around the screen. This is particularly useful if you are using a zoomed view.

- The **Changebar**, used at Publisher or Professional level, can be clicked on the **Property** button. This pulls out a new set of icons that can be used for making changes in whatever object is selected.

- There are **four varieties of Changebar pullout**, for text, graphics, pictures and frames.

- The Changebar **when no object is selected** offers file opening and saving, printing, automatic layout checking, and help from its icons.

66

8 Using WritePlus

Using WritePlus

WritePlus can be started in a variety of ways. You can click on the icon in the Status bar, or you can double-click on text on the screen page view. You can also use the Tools menu, selecting Add-ons and clicking on Write-Plus. Whichever method you use you will see the WritePlus screen appear with your text placed in it.

Take note

The cursor does not change when you press the Insert key, so you do not know if you are using Insert (the default) or Overtype mode. In Insert mode, whatever you type is added at the cursor position. In Overtype, your typing replaces existing text.

1 The normal cursor is a thick black line.

2 To select words or phrases, drag the cursor over them.

3 To apply font styles like Bold, Italic or Underline, to selected text, click on the appropriate button.

4 To select a paragraph, click on the name in the Style column (*soft.sty* in this example). To select the whole story, double-click on the name.

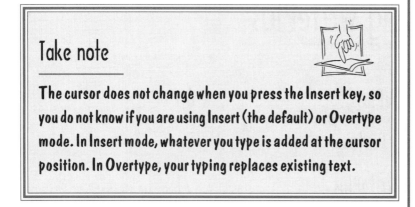

② Drag over to select

④ Style Column   **③** Text effects   **①** Cursor

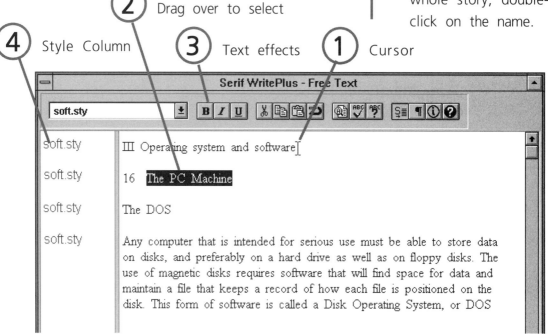

III Operating system and software

16 The PC Machine

The DOS

Any computer that is intended for serious use must be able to store data on disks, and preferably on a hard drive as well as on floppy disks. The use of magnetic disks requires software that will find space for data and maintain a file that keeps a record of how each file is positioned on the disk. This form of software is called a Disk Operating System, or DOS

Facilities

Making marks

1 Click on ¶ to see the codes in the text.

2 Spaces appear as • making it easy to spot excessive spacing.

3 Tabs appear as ».

4 The proof-reader's mark ¶ shows the end of a paragraph.

Getting information

5 Click ① to see the Info panel.

6 This shows word and character count, and displays the file name of the story.

Leaving WordPlus

7 Double-click the Control Menu button, or click once and then on Close.

8 Click ✓ to accept changes and return to page.

9 Click ✗ to discard changes and return to page.

WritePlus contains features of some very costly word-processor packages. Some of these are illustrated here.

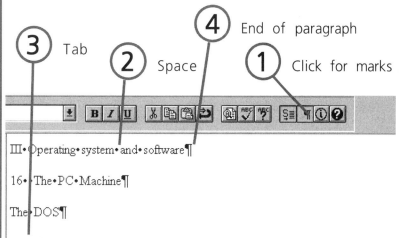

③ Tab

④ End of paragraph

② Space

① Click for marks

III•Operating•system•and•software¶

16•·The•PC•Machine¶

The·DOS¶

» Any•computer•that•is•intended•for•serious•use•must•be•able•to•store•data•on•disks,•and•preferably•on•a•hard•drive•as•well•as•on•floppy•disks.• The•use•of•magnetic•disks•requires•software•that•will•find•space•for•data• and•maintain•a•file•that•keeps•a•record•of•how•each•file•is•positioned•on• the•disk.•This•form•of•software•is•called•a•Disk•Operating•System,•or• DOS¤

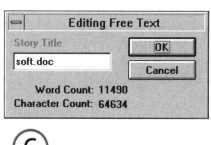

⑥ The info panel

Tip

Switch on these marks while editing imported text.

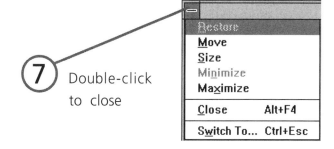

⑦ Double-click to close

Cut, Copy, Paste

Cut, Copy and Paste are standard DTP and word-processing facilities that are available from the menu when you are working in a page view. When you work in a page view it is difficult to see what you want to copy or cut, and where to paste it, and the alternatives are to use a magnified view or to use WritePlus. Since these actions should all be completed by the time you reach a page view, it is better to use WritePlus.

When you use Copy or Cut, the text that is stored in the Clipboard remains there until something else is copied or cut. You can therefore paste the same piece of text more than once.

Take note

You can use Copy, Cut and Paste, from the main page menu, applied to selected pictures or text in a selected frame.

1 Select the text you want to cut or copy.

2 Click ✄ to cut the text. The marked text will be deleted and stored in a piece of memory called the **Clipboard**.

3 Click 📋 to copy the text to the Clipboard without deleting it from its present position.

4 With the cursor placed where you want to insert text, click 📋 to copy the text from the Clipboard to the page.

5 Click ↩ (Undo) to reverse the most recent action if you have made a mistake.

① Select first

In addition to allowing files to be recorded, located and replayed, deleted and renamed, the DOS is extended to a large number of other actions, such as file copying, printer control, and monitor control. Before micro-computers became established, larger machines were using either specially-written DOS or using universal systems such as Unix or Pick. A one-off DOS requires all software to be written for that DOS, so that off-the-shelf software cannot be used, and so systems that allowed access to a wider range of software were

Tip

If in doubt, Copy rather than Cut - you can delete later.

Basic steps

1 If you do not see a Styles column, click on the styles icon ⌕. Click again to remove the styles column.

2 Click the arrowhead of the drop-down list to see the names of the available styles.

3 Click on a style name to use it for the selected paragraph.

4 The style name will appear in the styles column, and the text will take up the formatting of that style.

The default screen of WritePlus shows a left-hand column that is concerned with named Styles. This does not refer to the font styles or effects of Bold, Italic, Underline and so on, but to a combination of text effects that apply over a complete paragraph.

For example, you might, in a book, want to have headings that were in Arial 18-point bold, the main text in Times Roman 12-point normal, and some quotations in Times Roman Italic, indented right and left.

It would be tedious to go through a long piece of text making these changes, and WritePlus, like other leading word-processors, allows you to declare each combination as a style, with a name. Once this is done, you only have to assign a style name to each paragraph, and all the formatting of font and size, style, use of indents and so on, is done automatically.

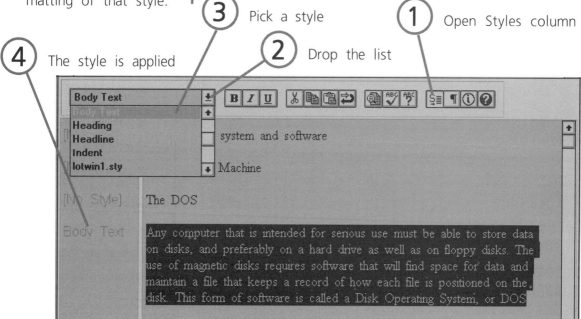

③ Pick a style

① Open Styles column

④ The style is applied

② Drop the list

Changing styles

Style creation cannot be done in WritePlus, and you must return to PagePlus to alter the list of styles that belongs to a publication. This is done from the Text menu, clicking on Text Styles, and then on Palette, or you can use the Styles button in the Changebar (extended version) after clicking the Properties button.

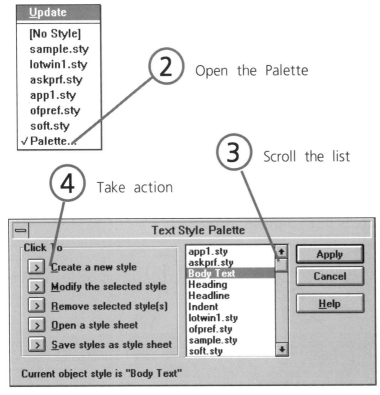

Update

[No Style]
sample.sty
lotwin1.sty
askprf.sty
app1.sty
ofpref.sty
soft.sty
√ Palette...

(2) Open the Palette

(3) Scroll the list

(4) Take action

Text Style Palette

Click To
> Create a new style
> Modify the selected style
> Remove selected style(s)
> Open a style sheet
> Save styles as style sheet

app1.sty
askprf.sty
Body Text
Heading
Headline
Indent
lotwin1.sty
ofpref.sty
sample.sty
soft.sty

Apply
Cancel
Help

Current object style is "Body Text"

1 With text on the page and the text tool in use, click on the **Text** menu and then on **Text Styles** (Professional level only).

2 Click on **Palette** to see what styles are available, and to alter them.

3 The style list appears in the Palette panel. Scroll the list to see the styles that are currently available.

4 A set of buttons allows you to **Create**, **Modify** or **Remove** a style or set of styles, and to **Open** or **Save** a style sheet (a file of named styles).

Take note

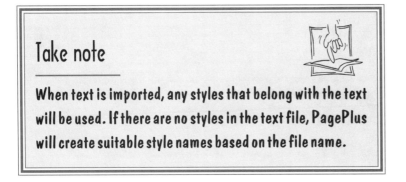

When text is imported, any styles that belong with the text will be used. If there are no styles in the text file, PagePlus will create suitable style names based on the file name.

Tip

If you think your styles are useful, save them as a style sheet that can be applied to other publications.

Actions

1 To modify a style, first click on the style name in the list.

2 Click on the action – **Modify** is shown here.

3 Click on the items you want to change – you return to this menu afterwards.

4 Click on **Save Styles as Style Sheet** and type in a name.

5 Click on the **OK** button to end the action.

You can edit your styles, or create new styles, using the Palette. Since the **Modify** and **Create** dialog boxes are identical, only **Modify** has been illustrated here. When creating, you start by typing a name for your new style.

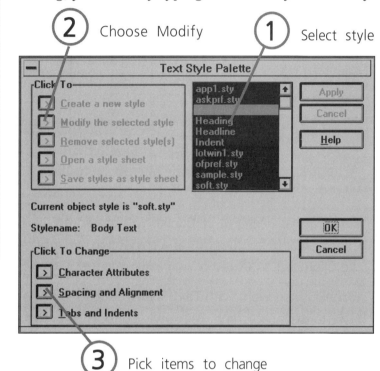

② Choose Modify   ① Select style

③ Pick items to change

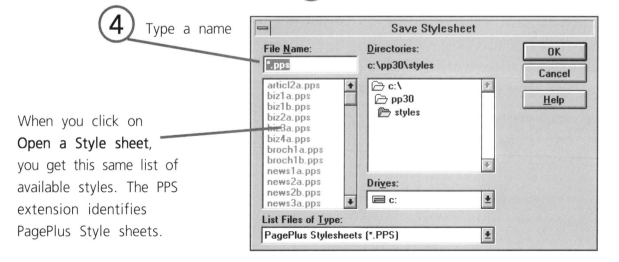

④ Type a name

When you click on **Open a Style sheet**, you get this same list of available styles. The PPS extension identifies PagePlus Style sheets.

Summary

❏ **WritePlus** is a very useful add-on for editing and creating text - it is particularly useful if you are working on text created by someone else.

❏ You can select text and **apply the usual effects** such as Bold, Italic and Underline.

❏ You can opt **to see the normally invisible codes** of space, tab and paragraph end. It is particularly useful to be able to see the paragraph end marks, because this mark shows the end of a text block.

❏ You can use the actions of **Copy**, **Cut** and **Paste** in WritePlus, to make larger-scale alterations to the text.

❏ Text that has been Cut or Copied will remain on the **Clipboard** until another Cut or Copy action, or until the Clipboard is cleared or you leave Windows

❏ WritePlus can work with **Text Styles**, allocating a style to each paragraph. Each style consists of properties such as font and size, tables and indents, etc.

❏ You can **apply a named style** to any paragraph by selecting it from the list in the Styles column of WritePlus.

❏ You can also **edit styles**, using the Text Styles option in the Text menu of PagePlus.

❏ You can modify an existing style or create a new one, delete a style, open a set of styles in a PPS file, or save your own set of styles in a file.

9 Text in bulk

Using the Thesaurus

A Thesaurus is a luxury that was not generally available on DTP programs at one time, and was scarce even on word-processing programs. The Thesaurus allows you to type a word and to query it, so that a list of suggested options will appear. One of these options might prove to be more appropriate, and if it is you can use it to replace the word you have typed.

Do not rely on the Thesaurus blindly. You need to know enough about the words you are using to recognise a good synonym. The Full Sense/Meaning section is helpful in this respect.

● *Make certain, before trying to use these bulk-text tools, that you are working at Professional level.*

Basic steps

1 With the cursor in the word that you want to replace, click on **Tools** and on **Thesaurus**.

2 The **Thesaurus** panel will appear - check that your **Entry** word is correct.

3 Select the **Sense** for the word that you want.

4 Select a **Synonym** (word with similar meaning).

5 Click on **Replace**.

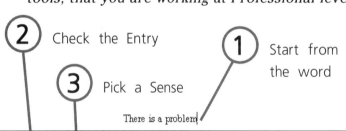

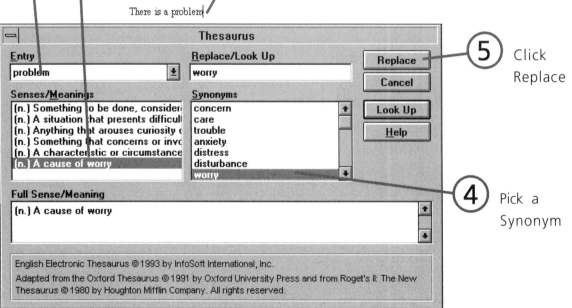

Basic steps

1 Put the text cursor at the start of your text.

2 Click on **Tools** then on **Check Spelling**

3 When a word is queried, the **Check Spelling** dialog box opens, and the word is highlighted in the text.

4 Pick a **Suggestion**, or correct it yourself, then click on **Change**.

5 **Change All** if you have made the same mistake several times.

6 **Ignore** to leave the word as it is.

7 **Ignore All** if there several occurrences of the same word .

8 **Add** to the dictionary, to store an unrecognised word that you will use again often.

Spelling Checker

Unlike the Thesaurus, which deals with one word each time it is called into action, the Spelling Checker will, once started, check all of the words in a story, or a selection of words if you opt for that.

Like the Thesaurus, the Spelling checker cannot be used blindly, because it will pass any word that is correctly spelled, even though the word is totally inappropriate. For example the phrase "a whelk inn the would" gets by because all the words are correctly spelled. The fact that the phrase is gibberish has nothing to do with it.

Choose if there are several suggestions

3 Queried word

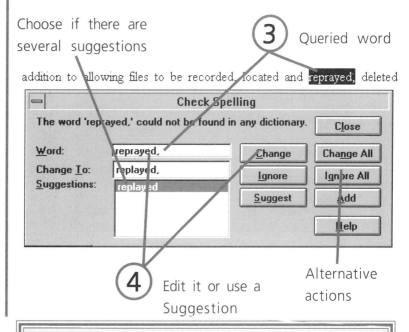

4 Edit it or use a Suggestion

Alternative actions

Take note

The Spelling Checker is not infallible. In the example, I might have intended to type 'resprayed', but this is not suggested. This is an example of an error that must be checked by hand.

Spellchecking hints

Since text that is to be checked is placed into WritePlus, it is often advantageous to start WritePlus on your text and then run Spelling Checker from within Write Plus.

Spelling Checker can be run from WritePlus by clicking the icon, and though the time required is much the same, using WritePlus offers you a better choice of the range to be checked. You can also opt for the QuickSpell check of a single word, see next page.

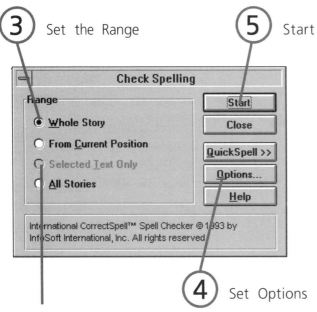

If you only want to spell check a block of text, drag the cursor over it to select it *before* calling up the checker.

1 Using the text cursor, double-click on the text.

2 When WritePlus shows your text, click on the Spelling Checker icon ▧.

3 Select the **Range**, from:

❑ **Whole Story** to check all of the text.

❑ **From Current Position** to check from the cursor position to the end.

❑ **Selected Text Only** if you want to check a block that you selected before starting the Checker.

❑ **All Stories** if you want to check work (such as a magazine) which contains more than one story.

4 Set ▨ **Options...** if any are relevant to the text.

5 Click ▨ **Start**

7 8

Spellcheck options

Whether you start the Spelling Checker from WritePlus or directly using the Tools menu, you will a find a button marked Options. Click this button to see the items you can ignore automatically in a spelling check. Clicking on the boxes, to put crosses in them, selects the types of words to be excluded from the checking process.

Repeated words, so you do not catch "too, too much", or a heading followed by the same word as the start of the next paragraph.

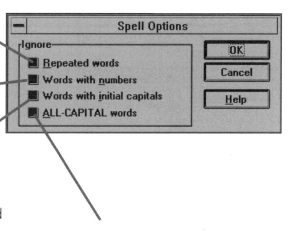

Words with numbers, so that you do not have to attend to Fig.1, Fig.2 and so on.

Words with initial capitals, so that names of people, places and the like are not questioned. Many of these are unlikely to be recognised, so this option is often worth setting.

Words that are in all capitals, such as DOS, NATO, UNESCO. This can backfire on you if you have used capitals to EMPHASISE words – a bad habit, as you can do it **far more** *effectively* by changing the style.

Tip

Use the Spelling Checker to find typing errors as well as spelling errors.

Quickspell

Quickspell is used to query the spelling of a word **before** you put it into a document. Even though you may be spell checking the whole document later, it makes to do this with words that you are unsure of. There is always the chance that Spell Checker cannot decipher your attempt at the word – and therefore not suggest a correct spelling. The way out of this impasse, is to use the Thesaurus to find an alternative word that you – and the Spell Checker – can recognise.

1 Invoke Quickspell from the Check Spelling dialog box. When the panel appears:

2 Type your guess at the word you want to use.

3 Click  and look at the suggestions that appear.

4 Click on the correct spelling.

(2) Type your best guess

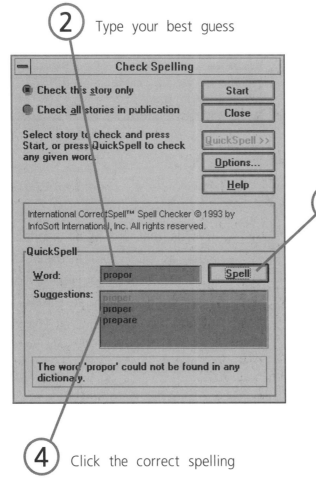

(3) Start it off

(4) Click the correct spelling

Tip

If you want to check a single word after you have typed it into your document, select it, then call up the Checker and set the Range to Selected Text Only.

Basic steps

1 Double-click on your text to start **WritePlus** (Professional level).

2 Click on the **Find and Replace** icon .

3 Type the word or phrase to find.

4 Type the replacement – skip this is you are just Finding.

5 Check the **Range** of text to search.

6 Select your matching **Options**.

7 Click **Find Next** to find the first place where the Find word or phrase appears.

8 Click **Replace** to replace this word or phrase.

9 Click **Replace All** if you want all occurrences of the word or phrase to be replaced. If not, use **Find Next** again.

Find and Replace

Find and Replace is a standard action for a word-processor, but has not been so common in DTP programs.

PagePlus allows you to carry out this action within WritePlus, making it easier, for example, to check text that has come from another author and which you want to revise before printing.

Find and Replace allows you to look for a word and (optionally) replace it by another one. For example, if your first attempt at a romantic novel took the world of airport booksellers by storm, you can find all the proper names (Audrey, Mark, Benley Hall, Twissleton Thorpe etc.) and replace them by others. The result is your second best-seller.

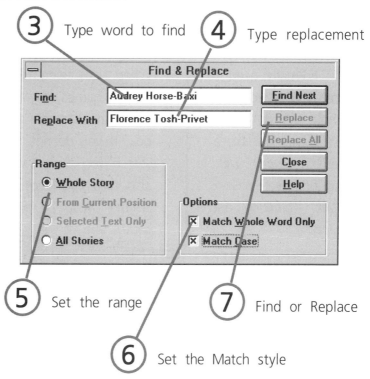

3 Type word to find **4** Type replacement

5 Set the range

6 Set the Match style

7 Find or Replace

Sundry Findings

You can start Find and Replace without using WritePlus. To do so, put the text cursor in your text and click on the Tools menu, then on Find and Replace. The Find & Replace panel will appear, but the options for searching text are confined to Check this Story and Check All Stories.

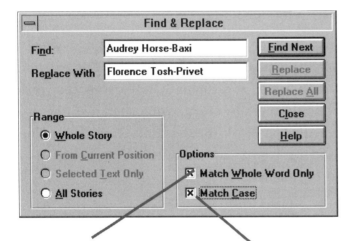

❑ You normally need to cross the **Match Whole Word Only** box. If you do not, a search for '*link*' will also find words like '*blink*', '*clinking*' and so on.

❑ When searching for proper names, always cross the **Match Case** box. If you do not, a search for '*Smith*' will also turn up '*black-smith*', '*smith*', '*silver-smith*' and so on.

❑ Be careful how you use **Replace All**. It is appropriate for the example of replacing proper names, but it can cause problems if you have not thought carefully, and particularly if you have not crossed **Whole Words Only**. For example, replacing '*co*' by '*co-*' (because you have just decided '*co-ordinate*' would be better than '*coordinate*') will result in words like '*co-w*' and '*co-ntra*'. A better choice would be to find '*coo*' and replace with '*co-o*', but even this is not foolproof.

Tip

You can often avoid problems of unwanted replacements with Find and Replace if you limit the scope of the search to a selected section of text.

WritePlus limitations

- ❑ Work in small pieces. Book are divided into chapters, so a chapter is a natural unit for a PagePlus file. Try to leave some free space in case you need to add material.

- ❑ Items like drawings and equations should be imported as objects, see Chapter 12.

- ❑ Watch your page numbering. Chapters usually start on an odd-numbered page. Carry forward your numbering from the end of one chapter to the start of the next.

The facilities that WritePlus adds to PagePlus are so considerable that you might be tempted to work on large publications, like full-length books. A novel is quite easy to set in this way, but you will encounter difficulties if you want to typeset works like technical, legal or medical books which would need an index and a table of contents. These can be set separately, working from page proofs, but you cannot generate them automatically.

Serif candidly point out that their own manual has had to be typed on a fully-featured word-processor (like Word-6 for Windows) which contains these features; it was then set using PagePlus. This latter process is not easy, because you cannot be quite certain that the page numbers in the word-processed version will correspond perfectly to the page numbers in the published version.

Remember the price difference between PagePlus and Word for Windows!

Indexing with Word

If you use Word-6 to prepare your text, you can index it with Word after your pages are set in PagePlus. Set Word to work with more words per page, and put in a hard page-break at each place where you have a page end in PagePlus. This way, the page numbers on the Word document should correspond with those of the PagePlus pages. You can then prepare an index, table of contents, figure table, or whatever you need. The index can be saved as a separate file and then input to PagePlus.

Summary

❏ The **Thesaurus** is a useful addition to PagePlus which is available at Professional level, either from a page view or when using WritePlus.

❏ You can **invoke the Thesaurus** just after typing a word, or during editing with the cursor on a word.

❏ You need to **select the meaning** that the word has in its context, and then choose one of the synonyms that will be offered. You can opt not to use any replacement if you so decide.

❏ The **Spelling Checker** can also be invoked from the page view or from WritePlus, but it always switches to WritePlus. Words are compared, one by one, with a dictionary list.

❏ You can opt to **ignore some types of words**, using the Options button of the Spell-checker.

❏ Remember that a word can be correctly spelled but be incorrect in meaning.

❏ The **Find and Replace** action is also available from the page view or from WritePlus.

❏ You can opt for finding, replacing after inspection, or automatic replacement.

❏ You can opt to ensure that only complete words are found and replaced, and that the use of capitals is the same as your Find word(s).

10 Drawing in PagePlus

Line drawing

You can use the built-in facilities of PagePlus to make simple drawings. If you need more elaborate drawings you have the choice of buying an expensive drawing package from which you can import files, or of using DrawPlus, a low-cost add-on for PagePlus.

At the time of writing, DrawPlus was being offered free, with a small charge for copying, post and packing.

Line drawing is the simplest action. If you hold down **[Shift]** and draw a line, it will be constrained in the same way as if you use the vertical/horizontal button action. You can draw a line anywhere on the page or the pasteboard, without using a frame. You can use such lines to separate pieces of text, for example.

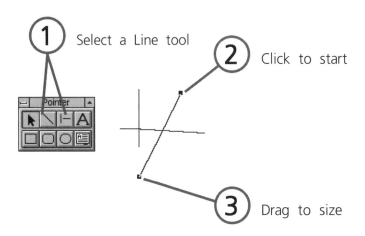

Select a Line tool

Click to start

Drag to size

Take note

You have to click the Tool each time you want to draw a line.

1 Click the straight-line drawing tool

OR

If you want to make a line that is precisely vertical, horizontal, or at 45° to vertical or horizontal, use ⊢ .

2 Click on the point where you want the line to start;

3 Drag the cursor to where you want it to end; then release the mouse button. The line will be selected with its 'handles' visible.

When a line is selected, you can click and drag on any part.

❏ **Dragging a handle** will move that end of the line, leaving the other end anchored.

❏ **Dragging any part of the line between the handles** will move the whole line.

Basic steps

1 Click the box tool 🔲

OR

Use 🔲 for a box with rounded corners.

2 Click on the point where you want one corner of the box.

3 Drag to the point where the opposite corner is to be placed.

❏ A box drawn over text will conceal the text with its fill colour.

❏ **To clear the fill**

4 Select the box

5 Click the Properties button on the Changebar.

6 Click the **Fill Colour** button 🔳.

8 Drop down the list, and select **Clear** as the fill colour. You will now see the text.

The Toolbox set of drawing tools offers the choice of boxes with sharp corners or with rounded corners. These are useful for containing text that you need to emphasise. You need to click the tool for each object you draw.

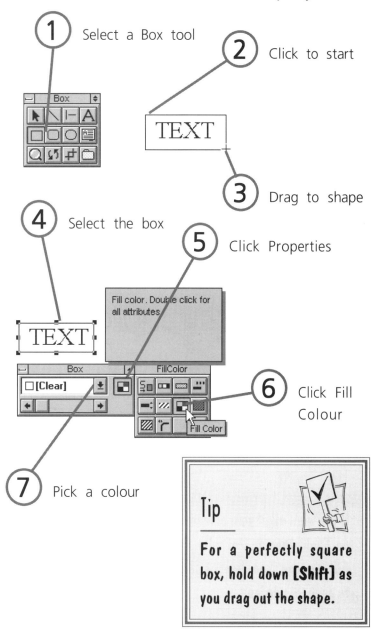

1 Select a Box tool

2 Click to start

TEXT

3 Drag to shape

4 Select the box

5 Click Properties

Fill color. Double click for all attributes

TEXT

6 Click Fill Colour

7 Pick a colour

Tip

For a perfectly square box, hold down **[Shift]** as you drag out the shape.

Circles and ovals

The circle and ovals tool allows you to draw these shapes and, like the box, they will have a default fill that will make them opaque.

If you hold down [**Shift**] while you drag the shape it will be a perfect circle, otherwise you can drag out an oval (ellipse) shape.

The shape that you see, however, until you release the mouse button, is a box - the corners of the box will be the positions for the selection handles for the oval.

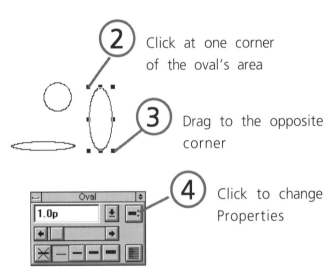

② Click at one corner of the oval's area

③ Drag to the opposite corner

④ Click to change Properties

1 Click on the Ovals tool in the toolbox [○].

2 Click at the point where one selection handle will appear.

3 Drag to the opposite corner to create an enclosing box.

4 If you want to alter filling, click on the properties button of the Changebar.

❑ See later, this Section, for altering line thickness.

Take note

You can make defaults of any of the properties of these shapes, not just fill colour. You need to click the Tool for each new shape.

Tip

If you want all of your closed shapes to have a clear fill, click on Tools, then on Defaults, Graphics, Selected Values, and Fill. You can then choose a clear fill as the default - remember to save this default.

Basic steps

1 Using ▶, click on the shape to select it.

2 Click the Changebar Properties button. This is always in the same place, though its shape will depend on what was last used.

3 To change the range of colours, double-click on the appropriate button, or on the colour fill button ▣ .

4 Select your action from the list. (For **Modify**, select the colour first.)

5 Select from the **Custom Color Selector**. OR

Specify the colour in terms of Red, Green, Blue content (**RGB**), or Cyan, Magenta, Yellow, White content (**CMYK**), or Hue, Saturation, and Luminance (**HSL**).

5 Name your colour and click on **OK**.

Changing colours

There are 35 standard colours that you can apply to either the Line or Fill of your drawings, and you can also create your own. If you want to do this, double-click on the button in the Properties box (Line or Fill colour).

Another option is to specify Pantone colours, but that choice is too advanced for this book.

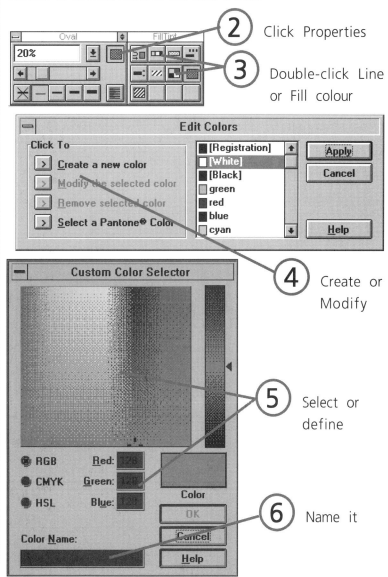

② Click Properties

③ Double-click Line or Fill colour

④ Create or Modify

⑤ Select or define

⑥ Name it

Shades

A property that relates to colour and can be applied either for line or fill of an object is shade (also called tint). Shade refers to the percentage of pure colour, because most colour are diluted with white.

A pure 100% yellow, for example, is a very strong colour, but at a 50% shade the yellow is paler, more pastel. The shade buttons on the properties box allow you to use these tints, and the default fill is 20% black, a light grey.

1 Select the object.

2 Click on the Properties button of the Changebar.

3 Click on the Fill Shade button

4 Either click on the arrowhead of the dropdown list and pick a percentage,

OR

5 Drag the slider to a new figure of percentage tint.

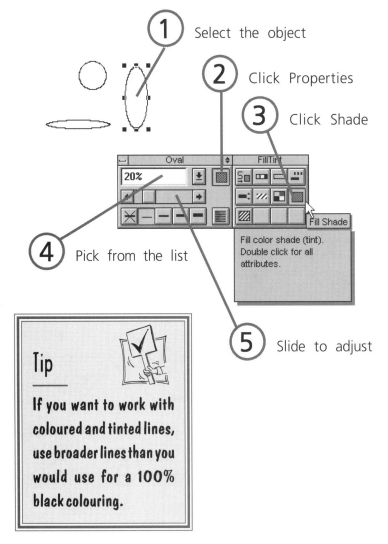

1 Select the object

2 Click Properties

3 Click Shade

4 Pick from the list

5 Slide to adjust

Fill color shade (tint). Double click for all attributes.

Tip

If you want to work with coloured and tinted lines, use broader lines than you would use for a 100% black colouring.

Take note

Colours and tints are still relevant even if you have no intention of printing in colour, because colours print as shades of grey. For example, lines with a low percentage of colour in their shading can be useful as background, like a watermark on paper.

Basic steps

❏ **Patterns**

1 Select the object and click on the Properties button as before.

2 Select the Line or Fill pattern button.

3 Select your pattern from the list of seven (including solid).

❏ **Line Weight**

This applies to all shapes, open or closed, and means the thickness of the line.

4 Select a line weight from the set of five on the Changebar (not in Intro level).

O R

5 Drag the slider to set the point size.

O R

6 Double-click on a line weight symbol to see the dialog box that allows you to change all the line attributes. This allows you to use dotted or dashed lines.

Patterns and line weights

The fill for a closed shape can be a pattern instead of a colour, and if your final output will be to a laser printer patterns are much better than shades, because a simple laser printer will not reproduce shades of colour as shades of grey.

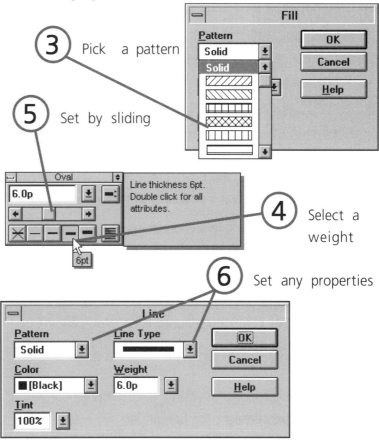

③ Pick a pattern

⑤ Set by sliding

④ Select a weight

⑥ Set any properties

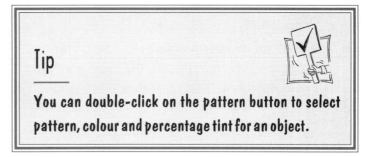

Tip

You can double-click on the pattern button to select pattern, colour and percentage tint for an object.

Summary

- ❑ You can draw **straight lines** by clicking on the appropriate button and dragging the cursor.

- ❑ A selected line has handle at each end. Drag these to can **change the length and angle** of the line.

- ❑ Drag between the handles to **move the line**.

- ❑ Holding down [Shift] while dragging out a new line will make the line horizontal, vertical or at 45°. There is also a button for this action.

- ❑ You can also draw **box shapes**, and these can be filled with colour. You can specify a **clear fill** if you want to see text in a box. Another button allows you to draw boxes with rounded corners. Hold [Shift] down to draw a perfectly square box.

- ❑ You can also draw **ovals** and **circles**, holding [Shift] down for a circle. As you draw them, these shapes look like boxes,.

- ❑ Closed objects can be **filled with colcur**, and all drawn shapes can use **coloured lines**. You can select from a range of colours, or specify a colour for yourself.

- ❑ You can also specify the percentage of pure colour, the **shade percentage**, for line or fill.

- ❑ Another option is **pattern**, selecting from a limited range.

- ❑ The lines for all drawn objects can be of different **weights**, and you can specify the line type (solid, dotted, dashed) as well as colour and shade.

11 Designing a flier

Where to start

Even for a comparatively simple publication, you have to know where to start. The world is full of bad examples, and a look around a few notice-boards will soon convince you that you need a few rules to work with. Good typographers don't need rules – just a lifetime of experience.

The guidelines are just common sense, but you will see notices and fliers all around you that leave you wondering when the event is, or what product is being sold at what price. The illustrations show the effect of flouting each guideline and so making the effort useless.

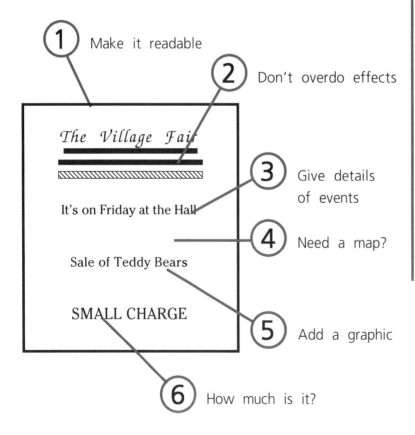

Guidelines

1 Make it **readable**. If it isn't readable, no-one will read it. Could you read this example from a car parked next to the notice-board?

2 **Don't overdo effects**, they just confuse the eye.

3 For **advertising an event**, state place, day, date and time.

4 Add a **sketchmap** if there is any doubt about location.

5 If you are pushing a **product**, use a sketch that gets the message over without words.

6 If there is no price, the reader will assume it's too expensive.

Guidelines

1 Make a rough sketch, preferably at the size you will want to use.

2 You might need to make more than one sketch. Go ahead - paper is cheap.

3 Make sure that you have incorporated all that is needed - the event, the time, date and place, map if needed.

4 If you cannot make a neat copy of a map, you may be able to scan a printed map, or make copies and stick them on. Watch out for copyright!

Rough sketches

Once you know roughly what you want, using PagePlus makes it easy to make the finished product.

You can waste an amazing amount of time on a project if you simply type words and then start arranging them on the screen to see what looks best. Take a look at the guidelines, left, to save yourself time and effort.

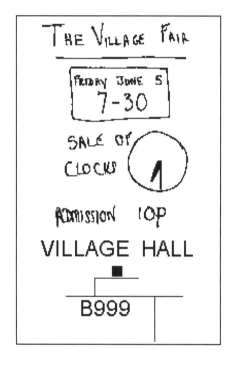

Tip

Work full-size if possible, and use a broad-tipped marker for writing - it will force you to write in a large size and not crowd too much in a line.

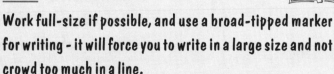

Starting a layout

The most intimidating sight for any writer or typographer is a blank page. By making a rough sketch, you have some idea of what you are going to put on that page.

- **Typefaces**. You might want to use one or two, but certainly not more than three on one page like this.

- **Type size**. If the notice is to be read from some distance, the lettering will need to be large. PagePlus fonts extend to 120 points, which is 1 2/3 inch high, but for larger sizes you can convert text into a graphics picture and make it larger still.

- **Effects** like underlining and boxes. The rough sketch suggests just one box.

- **Pictures**. In this example you will need the clock illustration and a map.

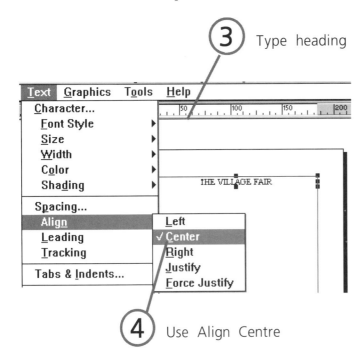

③ Type heading

④ Use Align Centre

1 For this form of work, prefer sans-serif typefaces. Start with just one, and think about others later.

2 The type size you can use depends on the page size. This can be larger than paper size, because you can make posters by tiling sheets together. You can also design and print on small sizes and use an enlarging photocopier for the final version.

3 Double-click with the text tool and type the heading.

4 Drag the block to the page, drag it to size, and centre the text.

Tip

Incorporating material from sources other than files is much easier if you have a scanner.

Basic steps

1 With the heading selected, choose a typeface and size. Try to use a size that will make the heading almost fill the width.

2 Switch back to the text tool and type the date and the time as separate paragraphs. Switch back to the pointer

3 Centre the date line and set its size.

4 Centre the time line, and increase its size - this can be larger.

5 Drag the handles so that the block outlines are close to the text, and drag the blocks close to each other.

6 Use ▣ to place a box around, but clear of the text

7 Use the Changebar, to thicken the box sides.

Developing a draft

The example used a size of 36 points initially and a Century Gothic typeface.

By clicking on the point size slider of the Changebar, this size can be gradually increased and you can watch it grow. Using menus, there is no size available between 36 point and 72 point, Using the Changebar, you can move in steps of fractions of a point up to the maximum size of 120 point that the Changebar provides.

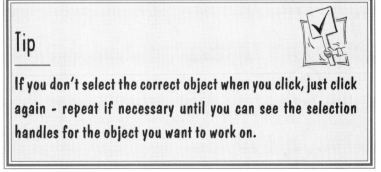

Tip

If you don't select the correct object when you click, just click again - repeat if necessary until you can see the selection handles for the object you want to work on.

Adding the picture

The picture is added using the steps that we have used earlier. In this case, there is no need to prepare a frame, just import the picture and drag it into the correct size and position.

All the other text is prepared a block at a time, and then the face and size are altered until the text looks suitable.

When the frame is created for the map, you can scan a map and import the resulting file, or you can draw a map in the space, using the drawing tools. Another option is to use DrawPlus if you have it.

THE VILLAGE FAIR

Friday June 30

7.30

Sale of CLOCKS

Admission 10p

① Import and drag to size

③ Type in and increase size

④ Add a frame

② Type text and set face and size

Basic steps

1 Import the picture from **Arts & Borders**. It will come in too large - drag it to a suitable size and position.

2 Prepare the text as a block, and select a suitable face and size. Drag the block so that the text is correctly positioned.

3 Type the text for the admission price, drag it to the correct place and increase the size by dragging the slider on the Changebar.

4 Create a frame in the remainder of the sheet so that a map can be inserted when you have a file ready.

Tip

If you want to use paper copies pasted in, make a box around your frame by selecting the frame, and using **Graphics Line**.

The difficult bit

1 Save the publication file, and print it.

2 Look at **fonts**. Is the main title big enough? Could it benefit from bold type? Is there too large a gap under the word SALE? Are the words in the box perhaps too large?

3 Look at **positions**. Is the text centred in the box? Is the box centred under the heading? Would the clock and text look better indented from the sides?

4 Once you have made up your mind on these issues, it's back to PagePlus to sort it out.

The next part of the work is the really difficult bit - you have to exert some critical judgement. Print out a proof copy, because it's easier to see mistakes on paper than on the screen.

You're on your own now, because what you think is a good layout is very much your own judgement. The important point is to try to look at the layout from the point of view of someone looking from a distance, some-one who has not seen it before. Ask yourself if the message comes across. If it does, 90% of your effort has been worthwhile. The remaining 10% is icing on the cake.

Tip

If you cannot move an object so that it is perfectly centred, turn snapping off until you have moved it.

Tip

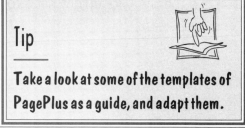

Take a look at some of the templates of PagePlus as a guide, and adapt them.

Summary

❏ Starting work on a layout can be daunting, and a few simple guidelines can help. The golden rule is to **avoid anything too elaborate at first**.

❏ A **rough sketch** on paper is very useful because it allows you to think about what you need to print and how it will be arranged.

❏ A **critical look** at the rough sketch can save you a considerable amount of time and effort later.

❏ You can then make a tentative **layout**. Type each line of text as a separate block, so that you can move your text around. For this type of work, drag the block sizes so that they are the width of the page, and centre the text.

❏ For more elaborate layouts you might want to use **guide lines** for positioning text and pictures.

❏ Use the **drawing tools** to create the box after the text has been centred. If you cannot centre the box by dragging, turn off snaps until the box is centred.

❏ There should always be a gap between text and an enclosing box.

❏ When you have created your PagePlus layout, print it and look at it critically.

❏ Now go back to PagePlus and finalise your layout.

❏ Keep the file - you might need to use it as a template.

12 Using objects

Text objects

PagePlus refers to objects, meaning units that can be manipulated. Manipulated in this sense means actions like moving, altering size, alignment, font and so on.

Three important types of objects are text objects, picture objects and frame objects, and many of the actions that apply to one will apply also to the others. We have already seen how the Changebar can be used and how its contents depend on the type of object that is selected.

In this section, we shall look in detail at how a text object is produced and how you can work with it.

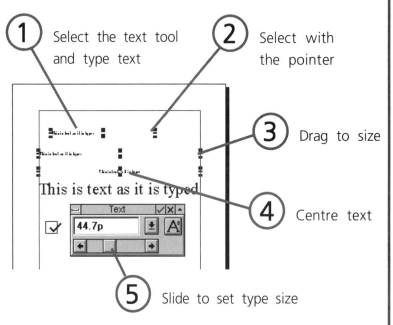

(1) Select the text tool and type text

(2) Select with the pointer

(3) Drag to size

(4) Centre text

This is text as it is typed

(5) Slide to set type size

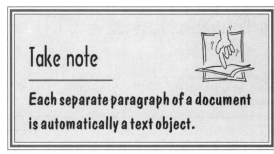

Take note

Each separate paragraph of a document is automatically a text object.

1 Select the text tool **A** and click on the page to place the cursor. Type a few words.

2 Change to the pointer tool **↖** and click to see the handles for this text object.

3 Drag the handles so that the text block is as wide as the page.

4 Use **Text - Align - Centre** (or the Changebar) to centre the text in its block. Since the block is of page width, this will also centre the text in the page.

5 Drag the slider of the Changebar to alter the text size.

❑ The text now fills the page width.

Object groups

Basic steps

1 Space the objects relative to each other exactly as you want them to remain.

2 Starting from well outside the (invisible) selection box for one object, drag the cursor so that a dotted box surrounds all of them.

3 Grey handles appear for all the objects, and you can now drag the whole group as one.

4 The objects remain grouped until you click on another object.

5 To add another object to the group hold down [Shift] and click on the other object.

The illustration shows three text objects, all of which use a full-width block and have been centred. This does not mean that the objects will look centred, and some sideways adjustment of one or more blocks will be needed to make the lines look centred relative to each other.

Suppose now that we want to move all three together, as moving them individually risks altering the spacing between them. This can be done if the objects are **grouped**.

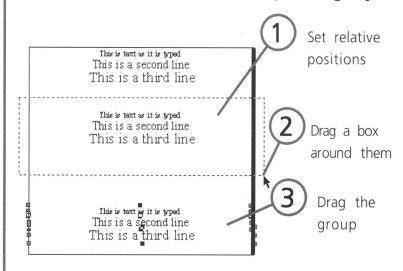

① Set relative positions

② Drag a box around them

③ Drag the group

Tip

If you want to put a grouped set of objects into a crowded page, compose them on the pasteboard, group them, and make them the last items placed on the page.

Tip

Grouping is an ideal way of keeping a picture and its caption together when moving them around. See later for converting a group to a picture.

Inside Wrap

Text can be made to wrap outside or inside another object, but you need to observe the rules carefully. The essential point to grasp is that each of the objects concerned must have a suitable wrap setting. For example, if you want to wrap text inside a circle, both the circle and the text must be given the correct wrap settings.

Failure to make both sets of wrappings is the usual cause of problems with wrapping text. Look first at an example of settings for a drawn object, in this case a circle. You can wrap inside, outside or not at all; round the selection box, or following the irregular shape of the object.

In this example, we have opted to wrap text inside the circle, and to make the text follow the shape of its rim.

1 Draw the circle and place it where you want it on the page. The text can be typed in a different place.

2 Use the pointer tool ▶ to select the circle.

3 Bring down the **Wrap Settings** panel from the **Tools** menu (or click the icon on the Changebar)

4 For this example, set **Wrap Inside**.

5 Set **Irregular Wrap**.

❑ The wrap appears as a dotted line.

3 Open Wrap Settings

4 Set Wrap inside

5 Set Irregular wrap

Wrap Settings

Status
- ○ Wrap off
- ○ Wrap outside
- ● Wrap inside

OK
Cancel
Help

Standoff
- Left 1.3 mm
- Top 1.3 mm
- Right 1.3 mm
- Bottom 1.3 mm

Outline Shape
- ● Irregular
- ○ Square

1 Draw a circle

2 Select it

1 Select the text. At this point it does not matter whether you have altered size or not.

2 Click on the **Wrap** button of the Changebar (or use the Tools menu).

3 Click on the appropriate wrap for this text, which is **Wrap around** or **inside**. Look for the QuickHelp panel to assist you in picking the correct button.

4 Drag the text to the circle and adjust its position.

5 If the text does not fill the circle, or if it overlaps, drag the text size slider in the Changebar until the text just fits.

Once the drawn object or picture has been set to wrap correctly, you can turn your attention to the text. Wrapping inside looks best when the text just fits inside the object, and this can be done by attending to the positioning of the text, so that the start of the text is at the top of the object, and also to the text size, dragging the bar in the Changebar until the text fits.

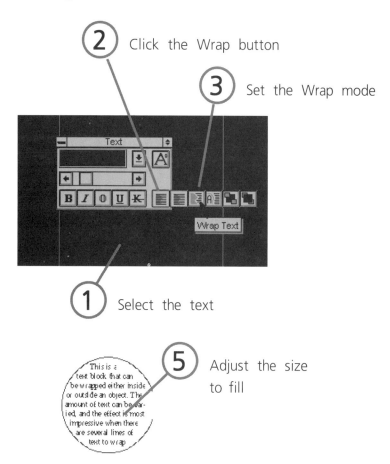

② Click the Wrap button

③ Set the Wrap mode

① Select the text

⑤ Adjust the size to fill

Outside wrap

You may want to wrap text around the outside of a drawn object. The steps are much the same as before, but with **Wrap outside** specified for the drawn object. The text is set to **Text will wrap**.

In this example, the drawing is a diamond shape that has been made up by rotating a square. You might be tempted to draw four diagonal lines and group them, but a grouped shape cannot have a wrap setting made.

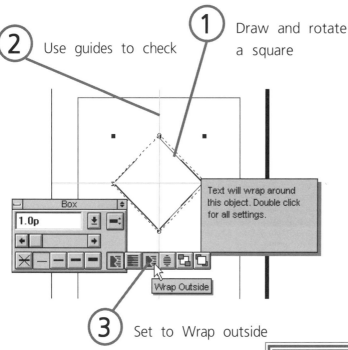

② Use guides to check

① Draw and rotate a square

Text will wrap around this object. Double click for all settings.

Box
1.0p

Wrap Outside

③ Set to Wrap outside

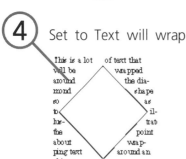

④ Set to Text will wrap

Basic steps

1 Draw a square and rotate it.

2 Click on the Ruler lines to make guidelines to ensure that your shape is a true diamond. Adjust the position of the shape and the lines as necessary. You may need to turn off Snapping temporarily.

3 Click on the Changebar properties button, and double-click on the **Wrap** button to set to **Wrap Outside, Irregular**.

4 Create text and set it to **Text will wrap**. Move the text to the shape, and watch it wrap outside.

Take Note

You cannot specify both Inside and Outside Wrap on the same object. If you want text in a box that is surrounded by other text you need to turn to other methods, see the next page.

Basic steps

1 Create an object, a box in this example, and place it on the page. Set it for **Wrap outside, straight edges**.

2 Set the fill for the box if you want to - the default is quite suitable.

3 Create the text and set it to wrap. Drag the text so that you can see it wrap around the box.

4 Create the extra text that you want to put inside the frame.

5 Adjust the text block and drag it into the box. Alter the size as required.

You may want to create a page which has a chunk of text contained inside a box, with the other text wrapping around the box. This needs a slight modification to the techniques that we have looked at in the previous pages, because you cannot set an object for wrapping both outside and inside.

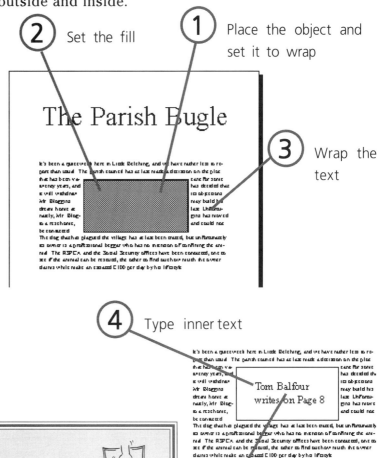

② Set the fill ① Place the object and set it to wrap

The Parish Bugle

③ Wrap the text

④ Type inner text

Tom Balfour writes on Page 8

⑤ Adjust the block to fit

Take note

If you make the inner text too large it will emerge from the box. If you want to make each line extend to the sides of the box, create each line as a separate block.

Changing the Wraps

When an object is selected and the Wrap options of Inside or Outside are used, a dotted outline appears to show the wrap boundaries. When Irregular Wrap is also selected, this boundary, instead of being a rectangle which is about the same as the selection box, will conform to the shape of the object.

You can edit this shape by dragging at the outline. The outline consists of a set of 'nodes', looking like bubbles, that can be dragged, and by clicking on the outline between nodes you can create additional nodes.

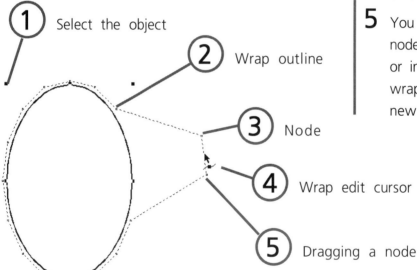

1 Select the object

2 Wrap outline

3 Node

4 Wrap edit cursor

5 Dragging a node

Basic steps

1 Select the shape - an oval is illustrated.

2 You can see the Wrap outline.

3 A typical node looks like this at this zoom level.

4 The cursor changes shape to its 'Wrap edit' shape.

5 You can click on a node and drag it out or in to make text wrapping follow a new outline.

Tip

This is a way of editing a wrap outline to follow a complicated shape, starting at the Wrap outline of the main object in a set. Remember that you cannot wrap a grouped set of shapes - but see Section 19 for conversion to picture.

Basic steps

❑ Copying

1 Press down **[Ctrl]** and click on the object.

2 Drag the object – only the outline moves.

3 Release the button to place the copy.

Cursors

⊕ **Move** cursor. Appears when the cursor is in a frame or block, or over a handle of a line.

⊘ **No move** possible. You have probably tried to move a framed object and the frame is locked. Check the **Page** menu, click on **Layout Tools** and look for the **Lock Frame** setting.

↔ ↕ **Alter size** cursors. You have clicked over a handle in the middle of a side. You can alter size in the directions indicated.

↖ **Alter size** cursor, as it appears when you click on a corner.

When an object has been selected, it can be copied or moved. You can click anywhere within the selection box to move an object (or a group of objects). You can move the object when the four-arrow type of cursor appears, but there are some exceptions for groups.

● Drag to move an object, holding down **[Shift]** if you want perfect vertical or horizontal movement.

● Hold **[Ctrl]** and drag to copy an object, using the cursor in the same way as for a move.

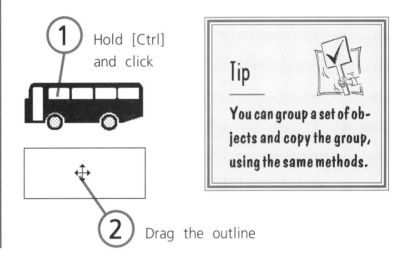

① Hold [Ctrl] and click

② Drag the outline

Tip

You can group a set of objects and copy the group, using the same methods.

Tip

If you want the copy directly under or directly to the side of the original you can release [Ctrl] as soon as you start dragging (when the outline appears) and press down [Shift] instead.

Size changes

Notes

When you carry out a re-sizing action on a selected object, you can (usually) modify the action by holding down either the Ctrl or the Shift keys. Precisely what the effect is depends on the nature of the object.

 [Shift] for regular figures

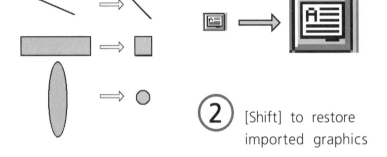

② [Shift] to restore imported graphics

④ Resizing text only affects the spacing

1 Pressing down **[Shift]** after you start a re-size action will have the same effect as creating the object with **[Shift]** selected. This applies to box and oval objects *only* if the re-sizing uses a corner handle.

2 If you resize an imported picture with **[Shift]** held down, the original aspect ratio (the ratio of width to height) will be restored. If it is altered, the proportions of the picture are distorted.

3 You cannot resize an object that has been rotated. Restore the object to its original angle first, re-size, then rotate again.

4 If you re-size **text objects**, you will alter the text spacing but not the size of the text.

Basic steps

1 Group the objects. Press **[Ctrl]-[A]** to make all of the objects on a page into a group, or group the objects in a more selective way. (See *Object groups*, page 103)

2 Click on the **Tools** menu and then on **Convert to Picture**.

3 After a short time you will see the grouped objects with a single frame and set of handles. This is now a picture and anything that you do with it must treat it as a picture.

The use of Grouping has been looked at earlier, but the snag was that a group is not permanent, it becomes undone as soon as the pointer is clicked anywhere else. PagePlus provides a way of making a grouping permanent, in the form of the Convert to Picture option in the Tools menu. The snag is that the change is irreversible - you cannot convert the object back to single items in any easy way.

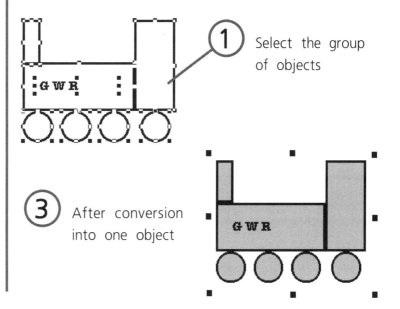

① Select the group of objects

③ After conversion into one object

Take note

The appearance of such a converted picture is often unsatisfactory on the screen, but it looks better in print.

Take note

The Convert to Picture option is greyed out if you do not have items grouped.

Summary

- ❏ PagePlus deals with **objects**. A paragraph of text, i.e. text that ends in a paragraph mark, is an object.

- ❏ The size and position of an object can be altered by dragging on the handles, using the pointer tool.

- ❏ A drawing object can be set to **wrap** inside, outside or not at all; a text object can be set to wrap or not wrap

- ❏ You can create **eye-catching effects** by wrapping text inside a drawn object.

- ❏ You can **wrap text around an object**. This may be a picture or drawing, or a rectangle which will have a photograph pasted into it later.

- ❏ You can place **text into a drawn object** when there is text flowing around it. You cannot make both the inside and outside text flow around an object.

- ❏ To **edit the Wrap outline** around an object, pull its **nodes** in or out. Click to create a new node. This allows you to wrap a grouped set.

- ❏ When **dragging an object**, watch the cursor shape. Moving occurs when the object is clicked between handles, re-sizing when a handle is clicked.

- ❏ Hold [Shift] after the move cursor has appeared to make a **move either vertically or horizontally**.

- ❏ Hold [Shift] while resizing drawing shapes (as when creating these shapes) to **preserve the aspect ratio**.

- ❏ Press [Ctrl] and the mouse button **to copy an object**. The copy is placed when you release the button.

- ❏ A group of objects can be converted to a picture, so that it can then be treated as one single object. This is done by creating the group and then clicking on the **Convert to Picture** option in the **Tools** menu.

13 Master pages

Headers and Footers

A header is text that is placed in the top margin of each page of a book, and a footer is text that is placed in the bottom margin. Common uses for headers and footers are book title, chapter title, page number, chapter number, page contents and so on.

PagePlus deals with headers and footers by using a Master page. A Master page is one that contains all the repeating parts of a page, the items that must appear on each page of a publication. You might create one Master page for a book, or one for each chapter, even one for each section of only a few pages.

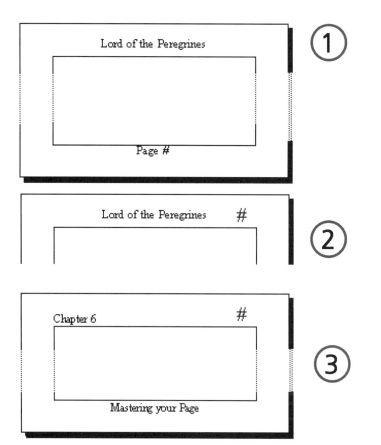

Layouts

1 A typical use of header and footer. The header carries the book title and the footer carries the page number. This appears as the # symbol until the pages are printed, when the actual number appears.

2 A style of Master page in which the page number appears prominently on the edge of the header, with no footer used.

3 Another format, with the main title as a footer and using Chapter number and page number in the header.

Tip

Take time to design your master page(s) - you will print a lot of them!

Starting a Master Page

1 Click on the **Page** menu and then on **Master Page**.

❏ You will see the Master page display with the darker pasteboard area.

2 Type the header text

3 Make the block full-width, and centre the text.

4 Change size and face to suit.

5 Drag the text to the header or footer space.

A Master Page starts with the Page menu like any other page. You type the text that you want, and move the text blocks to the header or footer space as required. Leave Snapping on so that the header or footer text is positioned just above or below the text area, respectively.

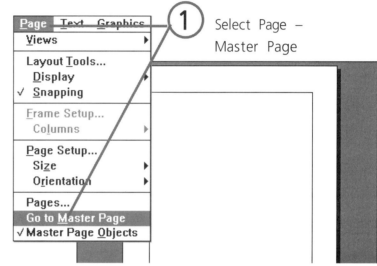

Select Page – Master Page

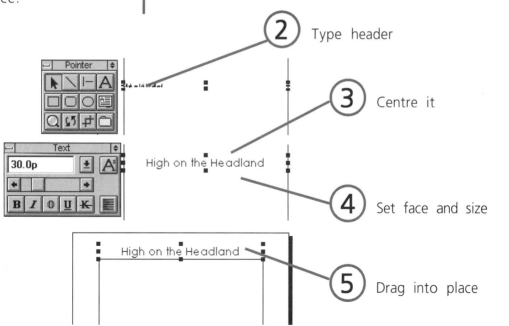

② Type header

③ Centre it

④ Set face and size

⑤ Drag into place

Page number style

Page numbering for a book is placed in a header or a footer, and you have to decide for yourself which to use. You also have to decide on the style of numbers, such as Arabic or Roman, lettering etc.

The normal convention is to use Arabic figures for all the main text pages, including any index. The pages that are called '*Prelims*', carrying title, publication data, foreword or preface, author's biography, and so on, are numbered using Roman numerals. If a Table of Contents is used, this appears in the Prelims.

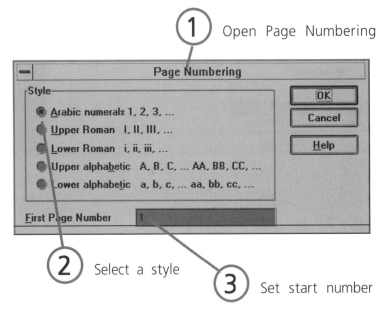

① Open Page Numbering

② Select a style

③ Set start number

1 You first need to decide on the style of numbering. Click on **Page**, then on **Setup**, then on **Numbering**.

The **Page Numbering** dialog box will appear.

2 Select from the choice of numbering styles - Arabic is the default; the others are upper or lower case Roman and upper or lower case lettering.

3 Type in the number to be used for the first page. The default is 1.

Tip

If you work chapter by chapter, which is advisable, note the final page number of each and use the next higher odd number for the start of the next chapter.

Take note

An convention for books is that each Chapter starts on a right-hand page, which carries an odd number

Basic steps

1 If you want to use text (such as '*Page*'), click the Text tool $\boxed{A}$ and type the word(s) - any point on the page will do at the moment.

2 Click on the **Text** menu and on **Insert Page Number**.

3 Use the Changebar to set the size of text - the illustration is exaggerated.

4 Drag out the block to fill the page width, and centre the text.

5 Drag the text into position.

Take note

The # sign will be replaced by the correct page number on the actual published pages.

Placing the Page Number

The usual positions for a page number are centred in the footer, or on the outside edge of a page in the footer or the header. Some users like the word 'Page' to appear also.

You do not type the page numbers on to a Master page. Instead, PagePlus will insert the hash symbol (#) wherever you want to place a page number.

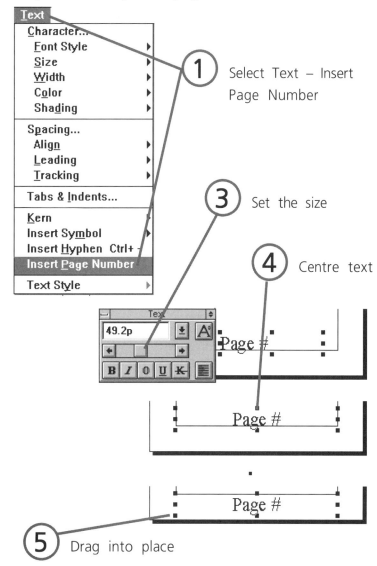

① Select Text – Insert Page Number

③ Set the size

④ Centre text

⑤ Drag into place

Double-side working

Pages for books are normally printed on both sides, with each new chapter starting on a right-hand (odd-numbered) page. This poses two problems for typesetting. One is that the page may need a larger margin on the bound edge, which is the left on an odd-numbered page and the right on an even. The other is that the page within the margins may differ if you want to place any part of a header of footer at the outside edge. Both points are dealt with by using two Master pages, one for odd and the other for even numbers.

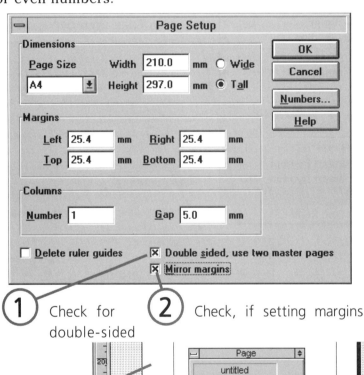

① Check for double-sided

② Check, if setting margins

⑤ Wider inner margin

Reminder that there is another Master page

⑥ On to the Left

Basic steps

1 Open the **Page Setup** dialog box and check **Double-sided**.

2 If you need a bigger margin on one side for binding, check **Mirror Margins** so opposite pages match.

3 Click on **Master Page**. A page appears, and the status bar shows it is the Right master.

4 Place a header and footer, with a page number if wanted. Remember to start with an odd number.

5 This page can be given a larger left-hand margin to allow for binding.

6 Click to go to the Left-hand master.

Notes

1 When you have completed a Master page, use the **Leave Master Page** option of the **Page** menu to revert to your normal page.

2 If you want a page to contain no header or footer, click on **MasterPage Objects** on the **Page** menu, to remove the tick. Click again to restore these.

3 When you start a publication, you can add pages with the **Page – Pages** option or by double-clicking the page number space in the status bar.

4 You can **add blank pages,** which will take the form of copies of the Master page(s).

5 You can also **add a copy** of the first page if you want several pages to be identical.

Two final points about Master pages:.

● With your Master page(s) prepared, you need to open the Page menu, and use the Leave Master Page option.

● You may not want a page number to appear on the first page of a chapter. This is dealt with on a page-by-page basis.

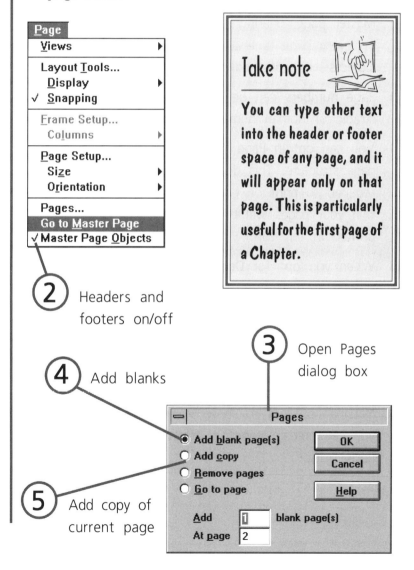

② Headers and footers on/off

④ Add blanks

③ Open Pages dialog box

⑤ Add copy of current page

Take note

You can type other text into the header or footer space of any page, and it will appear only on that page. This is particularly useful for the first page of a Chapter.

Summary

❑ You can make **Master pages** to carry material such as headers and footers that will appear on each page.

❑ The **Master page** option is on the **Page** menu.

❑ Virtually any form of header and footer can be used. The text is placed in the top and bottom margins

❑ You can place text anywhere else you want on a Master page, bearing in mind that such text appears on every page (unless you switch off **MasterPage Objects** on specified pages).

❑ **Page numbers** can be automatically inserted, using Arabic or Roman numbering, or lettering.

❑ You can opt in **Page Setup** to use Double-sided page structure. This does not mean that you are required to print on each side of each page, only that your pages will be intended to be finally printed in this form.

❑ When you opt for **Double-sided pages**, you must prepare two Masters, one for left-hand (even) page number, the other for right-hand (odd) pages.

❑ You can also opt for **Mirror Margins**, so that the larger side margin will always be to the inside, so making allowance for binding.

❑ You can opt not to show Master page items, and you can prepare pages in advance by using the **Add Page** option.

14 Further editing

Insertions

On some manuscripts you may find that you have to use special characters, like the copyright or trademark signs, in the text. PagePlus deals with this through its Text menu, using a section of Insert commands.

The Insert Symbol menu allows the insertion of Bullet, Dagger, Copyright, Register (trade mark in the UK), Em rule and Em space.

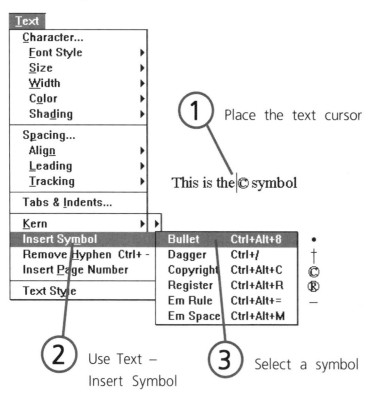

1 Place the text cursor

This is the © symbol

2 Use Text –
   Insert Symbol

3 Select a symbol

1 Place the cursor where you want the special character to appear.

2 Click the **Text** menu, then **Insert Symbol**.

3 Select the symbol.

4 You can also click on **Insert Hyphen** from the **Text** menu, when the cursor is between characters in a word.

❑ The word will not show any hyphen if it is not near the end of a line. If you do anything, such as altering face size, that requires splitting the word across lines, this is done at the hyphen position.

4 Use Text – Insert Hyphen

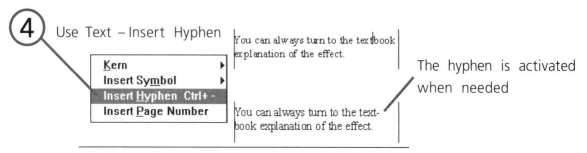

You can always turn to the textbook explanation of the effect.

You can always turn to the textbook explanation of the effect.

The hyphen is activated when needed

The Character Map

Basic steps

1 Click on the **Edit** menu, and then on **Character Map**.

2 Pick a font – Symbol, Terminal and Wing-dings are favourites.

3 Click on a character - you see a magnified view while you hold the button down.

4 Click on **Select** to put the character in the **Copy** box

Repeat 3 and 4 as needed.

5 Click on **Copy** to put the character(s) into your page.

The special characters that can be inserted from the **Text** menu **Insert** section are only a few of the characters that are special in the sense that they do not correspond to keys on the keyboard. The **Character Map** is a method of obtaining these and other characters.

Take note

The Character Map is part of Windows, not part of PagePlus. If you do not close the Character Map after use you can return to it with [Alt]-[Tab] in the usual Windows way. Do not forget to close the Map when you have finally done with it.

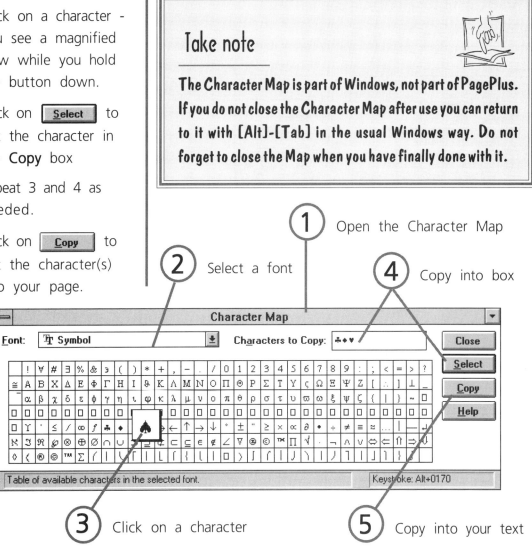

① Open the Character Map

② Select a font

④ Copy into box

③ Click on a character

⑤ Copy into your text

Inserting objects

Inserting objects is really a topic that belongs with using Windows, but because some Windows users have never required the action it is not as well known as it ought to be.

Basically, an object in this sense is anything that has been created by another program that is running under Windows, and the object can be a drawing, a piece of text, or a brief clip of sound (if you can use it).

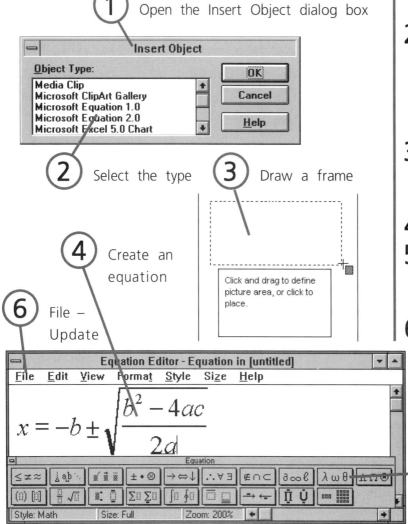

(1) Open the Insert Object dialog box

(2) Select the type

(3) Draw a frame

(4) Create an equation

(6) File – Update

(5) Use the toolbox as needed

1 With the cursor on a page, click on the **Edit** menu, and then on **Insert Object**. The titles you see in the **Insert Object** dialog box will depend on what programs you have available.

2 The use of Microsoft Equation 2.0 is shown here. Click on this, if you have it, then on the **OK** button.

3 You will be asked to define a frame for the object you will create.

4 Type an equation.

5 Symbols and effects are taken from a toolbox (press [**F2**]).

6 When the equation is complete, use **File – Update** to return to the page with the equation in place.

Notes

1 When an object has been embedded, and is selected, the **Edit** menu will carry an item that refers to the object. In the example, a Paintbrush picture has been embedded as an object, and is selected. The **Edit** menu carries the item **Edit Paintbrush Picture** as a result.

2 Use this option to start the Paintbrush program with the picture in place for editing.

3 The options of **Paste Special** and **Paste Format** are more specialised, and **Paste Special** in PagePlus is not used in the sense that it is in some other programs such as Word for Windows.

An object can only be inserted in this way if the program that creates it appears on the list when you use **Insert Object**. It effect is to start the program running so that you can create the drawing, text, equation, or other object, and to transfer a copy to your page when the program closes.

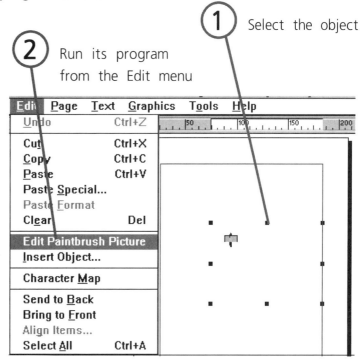

① Select the object

② Run its program from the Edit menu

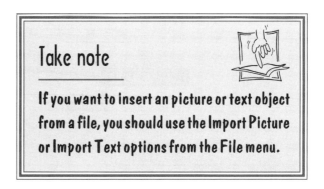

Take note

If you want to insert an picture or text object from a file, you should use the Import Picture or Import Text options from the File menu.

Layering

When two objects, such as drawings or text blocks, overlap, partly or completely, one is on a foreground layer and the other is on a background layer. We can alter a selected object's layer by using commands in the Edit menu (also in the Changebar).

These commands are particularly useful when you are working with objects that are not transparent, because they allow you to decide which parts of objects shall be visible. You may, for example, have created objects in an order that causes one object to hide another.

1 The two objects here overlap, with the text object in front of the box. Select the text.

2 Click the Wrap/Layer button on the Changebar to reveal the Send to Back and Bring to Front buttons.

3 Click on the **Send to Back** button to hide the text behind the drawn object.

4 Click on the **Bring to Front** button to make the text visible again.

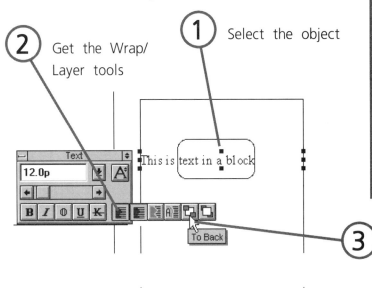

② Get the Wrap/ Layer tools

① Select the object

Text
12.0p

This is text in a block

To Back

③ Send it to the back

This is

④ Bring an obscured object to the front

To Front

Basic steps

1 Group the objects that are to be aligned. This includes text as well as drawing objects.

2 Click on the **Edit** menu and then on the **Align** option.

3 At the Align Items dialog box, decide whether you want vertical or horizontal alignment.

4 Select an alignment mode. The options are both described and illustrated in the dialog box.

Aligning objects refers to objects that have been grouped, so that the Alignment menu is pointless unless objects have first been grouped, and the Align option in the Edit menu is greyed out until the objects have been grouped.

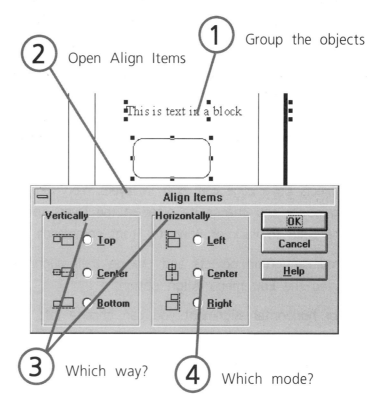

Take note

The Align option is obtained only from the Edit menu, not from the Toolbox or Changebar.

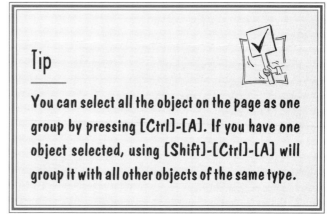

Tip

You can select all the object on the page as one group by pressing [Ctrl]-[A]. If you have one object selected, using [Shift]-[Ctrl]-[A] will group it with all other objects of the same type.

Summary

❑ You can insert some special characters into text by using the **Insert Symbol** option of the **Text** menu.

❑ For other unusual characters you can use the **Character Map**, which is part of Windows. This allows you to use a variety of typefaces, of which Symbol, Terminal and Wingdings are the most useful.

❑ The **Insert Object** option in the **Edit** menu allows you to embed objects that are created by other Windows programs. These embedded objects can be double-clicked to edit them using the program that created them.

❑ Objects on a page can exist in **layers**. You can select an object and change its place in the layers using the Send to Back or Bring to Front commands.

❑ You can group objects and change their alignment using the **Edit** menu **Align** option.

❑ For **horizontal alignment** you can choose left, centre or right alignment.

❑ For **vertical alignment** you can choose top, centre or bottom alignment.

15 Final production

Production

At some stage you need to give thought to what happens to your masterpiece after you have saved all the pages. The three items that concern you most are number of pages, number of copies, and complication.

The number of pages and number of copies obviously affects costs because these are based on the total number of sheets that are to be printed. Colour brings in another dimension of cost because of the added amount of processing that is needed.

In addition, using high-resolution artwork, such as photographs gummed into spaces that have been left in the pages, will increase costs, because you cannot then use the low-cost methods that are open to you when you are setting only text, or text with some line drawings.

Eventually, the big decision that you have to make is whether you do everything using a laser printer connected to your computer, or make use of commercial printing services for all or part of the work.

Ask yourself....

1 Do you need only a few copies, or are you talking about number of hundreds or thousands?

2 Is your publication a single page, a few pages, a booklet or a full-sized book?

3 Do you need to use colour?

4 Does your publication include high-resolution artwork?

Take note

No matter which way you choose, you must be certain that your work is 100% correct. This is particularly important if you are paying for several thousand copies in colour. No-one likes to scrap work, but that's the penalty of carelessness.

Examples

- ❏ Parish newsletters.
- ❏ Advertising leaflets for a small business.
- ❏ Business cards and compliments slips.
- ❏ Handouts for class tuition.
- ❏ Club newsletters.
- ❏ Catalogues for auction or other sales.
- ❏ Menus for restaurants.
- ❏ Personalised greetings cards.
- ❏ Headed notepaper.
- ❏ Order of service sheets.
- ❏ Invitations.
- ❏ Change of address leaflets.

Small-content work

There is a surprisingly large amount of printing work that can be done using PagePlus with a low-cost laser or ink-jet printer connected to your PC. For jobs that amount to 100 copies, or less, of a page, this should be the preferred method unless you have special requirements such as colour and/or high resolution.

This assumes that your printer is in good condition and is using suitable paper. If your work looks indistinct, smudged, badly lined up or with variable margins you will not be asked again.

For such work, you are totally responsible for setting and printing, and you should always ensure that someone else reads proof copies. The more the number of people who read proofs, the lower the chance of a mistake getting through. Never rely on an author to proof his/her own work. All authors read what they think they wrote, which is not always the same as the material they did write.

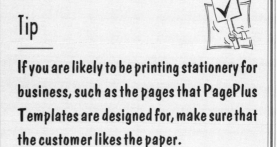

Tip

If you are likely to be printing stationery for business, such as the pages that PagePlus Templates are designed for, make sure that the customer likes the paper.

Outside services

You need outside services if the work is too much for desktop printing. If the numbers are too great, for example, you can use commercial photocopying services to turn out copies, and the price per copy will drop as the number increases.

Another route to high numbers of pages is to use your desk-top printer to make master copies that can be used as "camera-ready" copy for offset lithographic printing. This is expensive on a per-copy basis for small numbers, but much cheaper than photocoying for large numbers (several thousand copies).

The route that is required for really large numbers of pages, and for high-resolution work, is the use of PostScript files sent to a printing machine such as the Linotronic. Such machine are capable of resolutions of up to 2,400 dots per inch, as compared with the usual 300 dots per inch of a laser or inkjet printer, and they are essential if you need first-class reproduction of material that must be of razor-sharp clarity. If you want to use photographs they might need to be separately processed.

Options

1 Produce sheets that can be commercially photocopied.

2 Use camera-ready copy that was produced on your desktop printer.

3 Produce PostScript files for a Linotronic or similar printing machine.

Tip

Always ask! Do not rely on a printer to ask you what sort of files you are sending and how you want artwork dealt with.

1 For a small number of copies, and when high-resolution is not essential, a colour ink-jet may provide as much quality as you need. The quality of output from these machines is continually improving.

2 You can provide camera-ready output for spot colour printing. For each page that uses colour, you need to provide a page copy for each colour that you use, including black.

3 You can also provide colour separations, meaning that for each page using colour you need to provide four copies to make the four colours that are combined for the final print.

PagePlus was, from the outset, designed to provide the ability to use colour, and is still the lowest-cost way to working with colour. This, however, is not something for the total beginner.

Spot colour

There are two main ways in which PagePlus can add colour to your work. The simpler method is called 'spot colour', and it uses at least two print runs for each page that contains colour. One run prints the black (usually text), and another run on the same sheet then prints in another colour. You will use two sheets for each page, one with only the black copy and the other containing only the coloured copy. If you use two spot colours along with black, you will need three printing runs per sheet.

Colur separation

This option is needed if you are working with colour photographs or shades of colour. Each colour is analysed as a mixture of primary colours, and the most common system uses cyan, magenta and yellow along with a black/white copy. For such pages, you must provide a copy for each colour component.

Take note

PagePlus can make use of a U.S. standard system, Pantone ™, to specify colours. Check if your printer can use this.

Summary

❑ For small quantities of pages, you can use your own laser or inkjet printer to print all of your publication. A large amount of the need for printing comes into this class, and many large printing firms find this end of the market uneconomic.

❑ For more elaborate requirements, you will need at least some assistance from a commercial printer or typesetting bureau.

❑ You can arrange to have your printed copies photocopied, using a machine that produces better results than the usual office photocopier.

❑ You can deliver copy in the form of master sheets that can be copied by camera and reproduced by offset lithography. This is the most popular method for runs of around 1000 to 5000 copies.

❑ You can convert your PagePlus files into PostScript files for a printing machine, allowing much higher resolution to be used.

❑ For undemanding colour work you can use spot colour along with a colour inkjet printer to produce acceptable results.

❑ For 'glossy-magazine' colour you must use full colour separation methods and high-resolution printing.

16 Last words

Scanning

Scanning means passing a form of picture reader over an image, which can be a photograph, a drawing, or a page from a book, and obtaining from this action a file that you can use in your PC. This is a useful way of working with images because it allows you to convert the images into files that can be placed in your publications.

In addition, because these files can be edited, you can alter colours, shading and even shapes, or convert a suitable photo into a line drawing. You can add references with words or numbers to make the images easier to understand. With OCR software you can re-create books that have long been out of print, or work on a manuscript that has been sent in typed for rather than as a disk file.

PagePlus can be used with modern scanners that conform to a standard called TWAIN - your scanner should state that it is TWAIN-compliant. If so, you can click on the Picture Import option of PagePlus and see the Scanner option. Clicking on this will allow your scanner to be used, subject to the normal restrictions of that particular scanner.

Uses

1 To convert a photograph into a file that can be linked into a page.

2 To allow you to edit an image from a photograph or other sources, converting it into something that you can use.

3 To convert line drawings into images that can be bit-edited – you can also add text.

4 To scan typed or printed material and convert it into a text file, using **OCR** (Optical Character Recognition) software.

Tip

You may see curious messages when you use **PagePlus** with a scanner. In particular, there is one that ask you to choose one option or the other, but offers a Yes/No response. The scanning action is no problem, but you need a little experience with it.

How it works

1 The picture shows the underside of a hand scanner such as the Logitech ScanMan 32.

2 The roller moves as you pull the scanner down a page. Its movement is sensed and used to scroll the screen picture vertically.

3 As you move the scanner, a strip of tiny lights flashes in turn to illuminate each dot of a line of the picture.

4 A sensor converts the amount of reflected light (and its colour) into the numbers that are stored as a file.

> **Tip**
>
> **Use a scanner which will work under Windows - it makes life much easier, and it much more suited to using with PagePlus.**

Scanning hints

The hand scanner is the cheapest type and the one most commonly used. It is useful for small (up to 4" wide) and not too complicated images, but experience and care is needed to get images of a quality suitable for publication.

The full-page scanner is like a small photocopier, and usually takes an A4 page lying flat. Many scanners of this type can produce images that are entirely suitable for publication, and a few can work in colour. Prices can be very high if you want both colour and high resolution. This is ideal for high quality image work and OCR.

Roller type. The best-known example is the ScanMan PowerPlus, which looks like a pack of baking foil. It works with single pages up to A4, produces good images, and can be used with OCR. Prices are low, making this good value. It can be used for scanning magazines or books, but not so easily as with single pages.

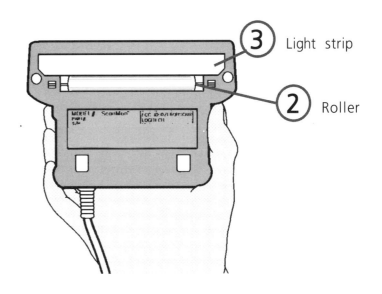

③ Light strip

② Roller

General Protection Faults

Windows 3.1 is a complicated system, and because no-one can predict what mixture of software you will be running, mysterious failures can happen which have very little to do with PagePlus, but are triggered because of a PagePlus action.

The most annoying type of failure is the **General Protection Fault** (GPF). You are happily working with PagePlus when suddenly a notice appears announcing a General Protection Fault. Your choice is usually quite simple – to click on the button that appears and so leave PagePlus. If you have not been using AutoSave, and have not saved your work in any other way, you will have lost everything you were working on.

Most problems arise because of the programs called 'drivers' which are used to operate the screen display and the printer. These programs are not written by Serif, and you may be using drivers which are not written by Microsoft either, because they have been provided by the suppliers of video cards or printer manufacturers.

Drivers can be in a separate directory, as in this set of video screen drivers, or located in the Windows/system directory.

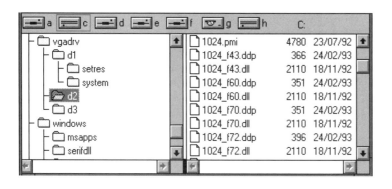

Take note

A GPF affects only one program, so that if you were running others at the time they will still be available. It is advisable, however, to save any files you were using in the other programs and shut down Windows altogether. When you re-start, you can start to look for causes of the GPF.

Tip

If you encounter problems with a video or printer driver, ask the manufacturer responsible if an update is available - this may cure the problem.

Avoiding problems

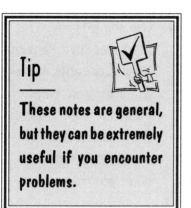
Use AutoSave. It may be annoying having to wait at intervals for the AutoSave action, but it can avoid loss of work. Power cuts can be more disruptive than GPFs.

Work only with TrueType fonts. This has the twin advantages of providing better printing and of avoiding a common GPF. If other types of Windows fonts become damaged they can cause PagePlus to display a GPF notice on start-up. By specifying only TrueType fonts you can avoid this.

Make sure that your printer driver is up to date, and is the one designed specifically for your printer. Never rely on 'emulations'. For example, if the manufacturer of your printer advises you that it can be used with an IBM ProPrinter driver, suspect this if problems arise. If your printer does not appear on the list that Windows provides for installation, contact the manufacturer for a suitable driver. If you are about to choose a printer, it's wise to look at the list of models that Windows can install.

The video card driver can cause programs when you print (so that you blame the printer driver). Suppliers of video cards all supply drivers, which can cause problems because no-one can try every combination of software with them. Try one of the standard Windows VGA drivers, and if this solves your problems, stay with it.

Check the README file of PagePlus 3.0 for examples of problems. Print out this file and read it at leisure, because it provides a large number of solutions to problems that have been encountered in the past.

Getting Help

When you make use of any program at first, you often need help, and you cannot always work with the manual in one hand. The on-line help that PagePlus offers can be very useful. You can find this Help by using the **[F1]** key, from the Help menu, or from the Changebar (with nothing selected).

1 Use the **[F1]** key. This produces the PagePlus **Help Contents** panel, as illustrated below. You can then click on the button that describes the type of help you need.

2 Click on the **Help** menu. This produces the usual menu display from which you can pick the type of Help that you want.

3 Click the question-mark button 🔘 on the Changebar when this is visible. You will see the PagePlus Help Contents display.

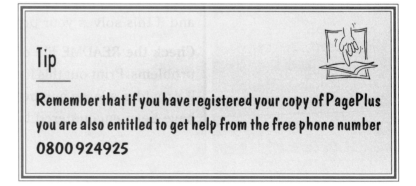

Tip

Remember that if you have registered your copy of PagePlus you are also entitled to get help from the free phone number **0800 924 925**

Advantages

1 You can get advice from someone who has probably come across the same difficulty.

2 You are likely to be speaking to someone who has experience of dealing with printing firms and preparation bureaux as well as with PagePlus.

3 The number is not a premium one, so that you are charged at normal rate.

4 Like other user groups, the PagePlus group publishes a newsletter, and you can often find information that will avoid a problem which otherwise would have required help.

Every good piece of software causes a User Group to be built up, and PagePlus is no exception. As the name suggests, the group consists of users of PagePlus, people who have come across all sorts of tips and quirks and who are eager to share their knowledge and experience with you.

The User Group, unusually among such groups, also undertakes training, either at your location or theirs. Advertisements appear regularly in the PC computer press. The telephone number at the time of writing is: 01526 834698

Summary

❏ A **scanner** is a useful and natural companion to PagePlus, because it greatly increases your ability to work with images.

❏ The scanner can work on mixed text and image pages, and you can **edit the files** that it produces.

❏ If the scanner can make use of **OCR software**, you can convert old printed matter or typed material into a text file that PagePlus and other programs can use.

❏ **Hand scanners** are useful, but their 4 inch (100 mm) width restricts their use, even when the software permits scanning in several strips.

❏ The full-page **flat-bed scanner** can produce excellent results, with high resolution and, if required, colour, but the most able types are expensive.

❏ The latest **roller type** of scanner is an excellent compromise,and performs well with images or OCR.

❏ **General Protection Faults** can occur when using PagePlus. They are caused by problems within Windows, and can be reduced by using the correct video and printer drivers, and only True Type fonts.

❏ There are three main ways of obtaining **Help** for PagePlus by using the [F1] key, by using the **Help** menu, or by using the icon in the Changebar.

❏ If you cannot find what you want in the manual or in the on-screen Help, the freephone number for **registered** users will answer your questions.

❏ You can also obtain help and tuition from the **PagePlus User Group**.

Index